Furniture Makers Exploring Digital Technologies

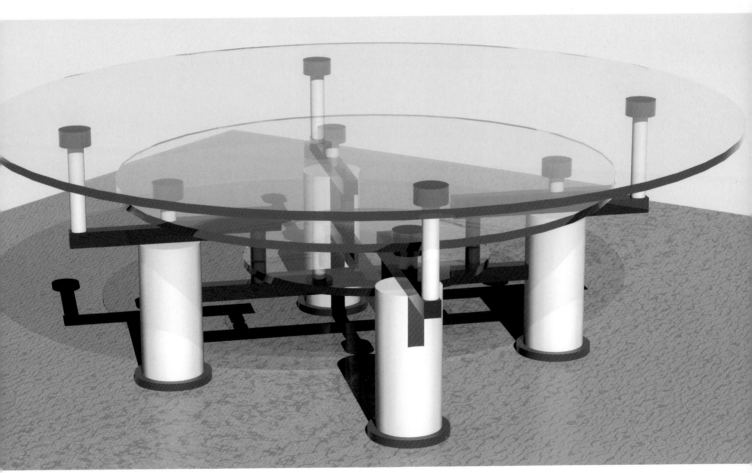

Digital drawing for *3-Tier Cocktail Table* by Romeu-Richard Furniture. For the table as built, see page 17.

Bench by Aaron Reed of Savannah, GA, won the nod of the visiting critic in the member's gallery at The Furniture Society's 2004 conference. It measures 65 inches by 24 inches by 20 inches. The understructure and depth-wise seat extension are made of welded steel, the seat is a cypress stair tread that Reed salvaged from a railroad station renovation. Though he is adept with digital processes, Reed says the finished bench popped into focus the instant he found that cypress plank.

FURNITURE STUDIO 3

Furniture Makers Exploring Digital Technologies

ANNUAL JOURNAL OF THE FURNITURE SOCIETY

The Furniture Society

The Furniture Society is a non-profit organization
whose mission is to advance the art of furniture making
by inspiring creativity, promoting excellence, and fostering
understanding of this art and its place in society.

Furniture Studio 3
Furniture Makers Exploring Digital Technologies
ISBN 0-9671004-2-9
Copyright © 2005 by The Furniture Society
All rights reserved

Editor: John Kelsey
Design and layout: Maura J. Zimmer
Copy editor: Kate Garrenson

Editorial Board of Advisors:

Miguel Gomez-Ibanez, President, The Furniture Society; architect and furniture maker, Weston, MA.

Dennis FitzGerald, furniture maker; coordinator of woodworking and furniture design,
    State University of New York, Purchase NY.

Ashley Jameson Eriksmoen, furniture designer and maker, Oakland, CA.

Dr. Oscar P. Fitzgerald, faculty member, Smithsonian Institution/Parsons School
    Master's Program in the Decorative Arts.

Richard S. Newman, furniture designer and maker, Rochester, NY.

Michael S. Podmaniczy, furniture maker; senior conservator, Winterthur Museum.

Printed in China

First printing: September 2005

Library of Congress Cataloging-in-Publication Data

Furniture makers exploring digital technologies / edited by John Kelsey.
    p. cm. – (Furniture studio ; 3)
  Includes index.
  ISBN 0-9671004-2-9
1. Furniture design–United States–History–20th century. 2. Furniture design–United States–History-
-21st century. 3. Furniture design–Data processing. 4. Functionalism in art. I. Kelsey, John, 1946- II.
Series.
  NK2408.F88 2005
  749'.0973'09049–dc22

                    2005009502

THE FURNITURE SOCIETY
111 Grovewood Road
Asheville, NC 28801
Phone: 828-255-1949; fax 828-255-1950
www.furnituresociety.org

Rights inquiries: Book trade orders:
Cambium Press   Independent Publishers Group (IPG)
PO Box 909   814 North Franklin St.
Bethel, CT 06801   Chicago, IL 60610
www.cambiumpress.biz   312-337-0747 fax 312-337-5985
                                  www.ipgbook.com

Preface

Embracing Technology—Honoring Tradition was the theme of the Furniture Society's 2004 conference, and the energy created by this subject led us to the subject of this third volume in the *Furniture Studio* series, *Furniture Makers Exploring Digital Technologies*. Many of the essays expand upon exhibitions and presentations at the conference, others result from our ongoing effort to showcase new work and expand critical writing on the subject of studio furniture.

By its very breadth the field of studio furniture transcends the narrow, media-based definitions that are customary in the craft world. This diversity shifts the discussion away from materials and techniques and into the larger context of culture and ideas. While advanced technology is the overall theme, the art of making furniture is old, diverse and growing, so traditional techniques and forms are discussed as well.

The *Furniture Studio* series of books is now an annual benefit of membership in The Furniture Society. The expansion of our publishing program has been made possible by a generous grant, given anonymously. On behalf of The Furniture Society, I want to thank the donors for their steadfast support of our field, as well as for their ongoing contributions to our organization.

It gives me great pleasure to dedicate this volume to the members of The Furniture Society, in the hope and expectation that the words and photos presented here will enrich their professional lives. Thank you for your ongoing involvement, support and encouragement.

—*Andrew H. Glasgow, Executive Director*

Furniture Studio, the annual journal of The Furniture Society, chronicles the work and interests of people who make studio furniture. There are at least three good ways to become involved in this publishing project.

Show your work to the world. When you place your work in shows, sales, conferences, and exhibitions sponsored by The Furniture Society and other organizations active in the field, you also bring it to the attention of colleagues, collectors, curators, and writers. *Furniture Studio* draws heavily on Furniture Society activities for its editorial material.

Show us your work. Please send a sheet of slides, or a CD of digital images (preferably 300 dpi RGB), of your recent furniture to the editors. We're always looking for new and interesting pieces to feature in *Furniture Studio*.

Participate in this publishing project. Propose to write an article for publication in *Furniture Studio*. The broader your idea, and the more new work it includes by makers other than yourself, the more likely your proposed article will be of general interest.

Please send publicity material, images, and article ideas to Furniture Studio, PO Box 909, Bethel, CT 06801. Thank you!

—*John Kelsey, editor*

Mission

Furniture Studio, the annual journal of The Furniture Society, presents images and ideas about studio furniture, furniture making and design, and furniture makers/artists. By placing studio furniture in an artistic, social, cultural, and historical context, the journal promotes a better understanding of the work and inspires continuing advancement in the art of furniture making.

Policy

It is the editorial policy of *Furniture Studio* to represent all aspects of the studio furniture field, reflecting its diversity as to age, gender, materials, and stylistic preference. A broad range of connoisseurs, writers, critics, and historians from within and outside the field offers reflection and opinion in the journal. The journal encourages the work of emerging designers, makers, and writers.

Mission and policy statement adopted by The Furniture Society Editorial Advisory Board, May 2004

p. 8

p. 20

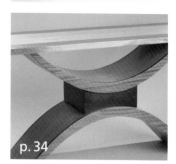

p. 34

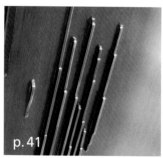

p. 41

p. 48

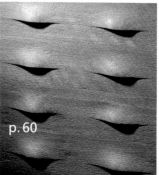

p. 60

Contents

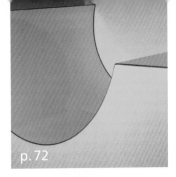

p.72

p.86

p.92

Reviews

p.106

p.111

p.118

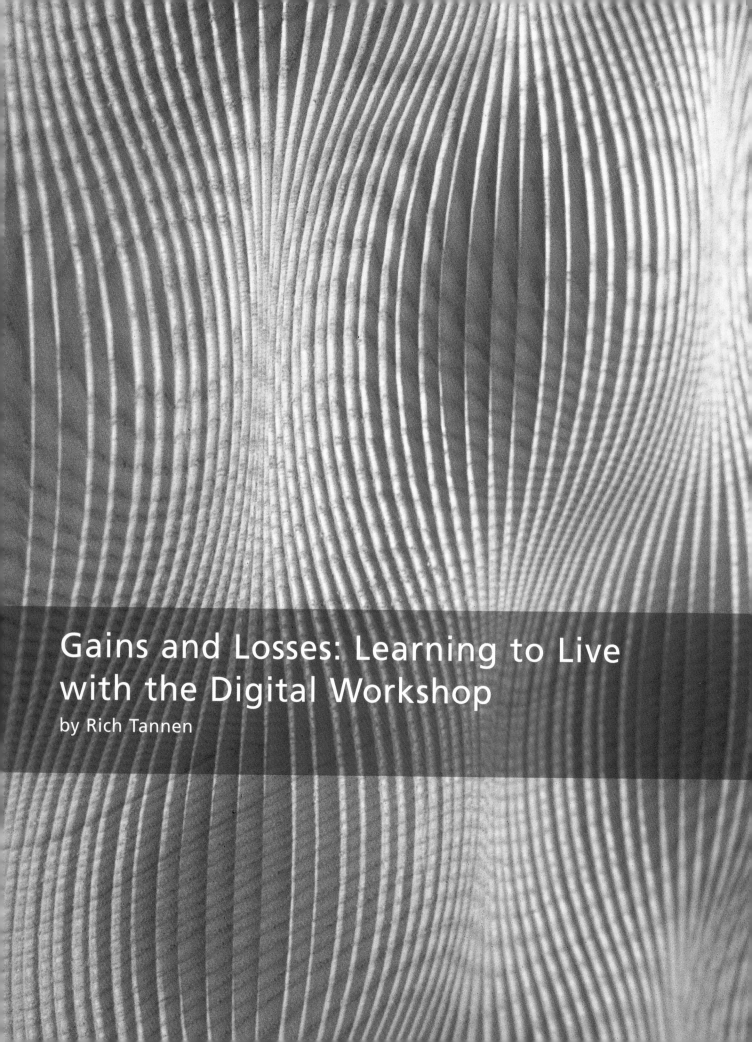

Gains and Losses: Learning to Live with the Digital Workshop

by Rich Tannen

New technologies supplement traditional work by hand and machine, but they're not a substitute

All technology encourages some behaviors and inhibits others. A maker with only a table saw does well if he or she is making things with straight lines. A decision to introduce curves creates a dilemma: either find a way to create those curves, or give up on them. Similarly, a person with only a band saw will thrive if their ambitions include curves—straight lines become the challenge. One could argue that the wise maker will have both a band saw and a table saw so that their vision is not tainted by the natural preferences expressed by the technology. This sounds simple enough. In a related example, we might ask three students to design a piece of furniture and represent their designs in model form. One student is given clay, one is given foamcore, and the third is given three-dimensional computer software. We expect their results to be influenced by these three different processes. In the table saw/band saw example, we hope the idea comes first and the best way to realize it follows. In the student design example we see that the process inevitably does influence the idea. We need to be sure we remain aware and sensitive to this and that we choose our methods wisely.

These simple examples concern the nature of the relationship between one's vision for the work and the means by which it is realized. The vision central to this discussion encompasses the entire process from conception, to production, and reception. It defines the work and helps give it cultural context. I teach in a crafts school where I have introduced the opportunity to engage in digital technology in the form of CADD (Computer-Aided Design and Drafting) and CAM (Computer-Aided Manufacturing) to the curriculum. I am also a studio furniture-maker, and I have, in recent years, experimented with CADD and CAM in my own work, both conceptually and as a means of manufacture.

Rich Tannen is a professor in the wood program at the School of American Crafts, Rochester (NY) Institute of Technology. He presented a version of this paper during the critical discourse panel at The Furniture Society's Savannah conference in June 2004.

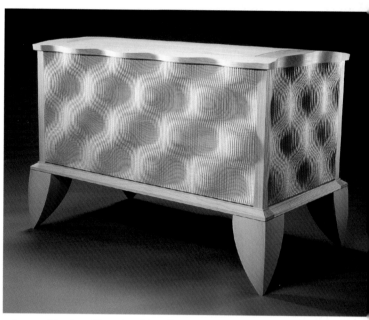

above: *Blanket Chest* by Rich Tannen, ash with lacquer finish, 37 inches x 20 inches x 24 inches high. Photo by Geoff Tesch.

left: Detail of blanket chest shows the texture created by the CNC machine, which the artist chose to emphasize rather than to eliminate. Photo by Geoff Tesch.

Ten years ago I introduced a CADD component to our architectural drafting course, not to replace paper-and-pencil training, but to supplement it. This innocent and modest foray into the digital world became a slippery slope that I have negotiated mostly through trial and error. Right now, digital technology is nipping at the edges of our curriculum. As a school we have not yet satisfactorily confronted these new, transformative tools, but in the professional world of design, CADD has become ubiquitous. Anyone who has experienced the power and potential of CADD can understand why. Designers use drawing as a principle tool in the creation of their vision and to communicate their intentions to those who produce their designs. CADD is replacing hand-drawing in architecture, industrial design, and interior design for much, if not all but the most basic, conceptual sketching. This is happening often without rigorous analysis as to what is being gained and lost. It is a

As exciting as the experience of employing the digital technology was, I also experienced a troubling isolation from the material and the act of making.

complex problem because CADD's power blurs the distinctions between designing and drafting, and between developmental drawing and drafted presentation or working drawings.

The fundamental principles underlying the relationship between design, drawing, and the ways in which drawing can be used to develop ideas become more important than ever. For the untrained or unsophisticated user CADD software has all the knowledge necessary to leapfrog past those principles. Take perspective drawing, for example, which CADD can accomplish because perspective drawing is a mathematical construct embedded in its own structure. The discussion of converging lines need no longer take place. What about the concept of the observer's relative position to the object being observed? What about the cone of vision, outside of which objects become distorted, and what of the intuitive relationship this has to peripheral vision and to how we really see the world? What about a sense of scale? We come to better understand these concepts by learning how to draw in perspective. Embedded in learning these technical skills are ideas that inform us as thinkers, designers, and makers. Our understanding of these ideas can erode over time and be replaced by new technologies. Our knowledge can be replaced by the information the computer provides.

Laurie Olin, a landscape architect and former chair of the Landscape Architecture Department at Harvard's Graduate School of Design, has this to say on the subject of drawing: "After viewing some remarkable computer studies underway at the GSD, a friend and distinguished city planner turned to me and said, 'Laurie, is there going to be any use for pencils in the future of architecture?' I believed the obvious answer was, 'Yes, of course!' I am as certain of that now as I was at the moment, but I am still puzzled as to how to explain to her and to other intelligent people what the relationship between seeing, thinking and drawing is; how, despite the

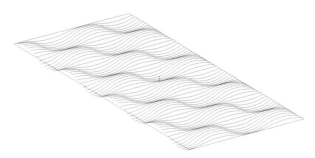

Screen capture shows the mathematical surface rendered in the wooden panels of the blanket chest.

achievements of people with computers, for those with a visual imagination and adequate preparation, they are as unlikely to be a real substitute for drawing as they are for the use of words and language. …It appears that among the young people now at work in offices across the country and abroad, those who understand and are well-trained in traditional drawing generally make the most of computer graphics and design studies. While complaining about a particularly stiff and uncommunicative computer drawing, Bruce Graham, of Skidmore, Owings and Merrill, turned to me and remarked that the people who were most sensitive to line weight, nuances of color, and graphic problems in drawing also produced the most elegant work with computers, and vice versa." (Olin 1996)

Like the designer, a craftsperson uses drawing to develop the vision for their work, but, unlike the designer, a craftsperson is also the maker, so they need only communicate their intentions to themselves (I am leaving presentation to clients out of this discussion). There is no need for uniformity in how this communication is accomplished. Some craftspeople use CADD, some create working drawings by hand, drawing in sketchbooks, on the back of napkins, or on the material itself. Any of

CADD: *Computer-Aided Design and Drafting*

CAM: *Computer-Aided Manufacturing*

CNC: *Computer Numerical Control*

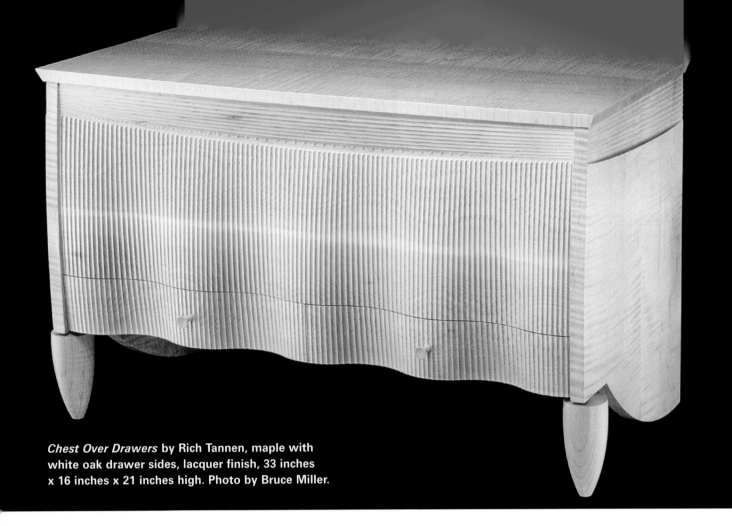

Chest Over Drawers by Rich Tannen, maple with white oak drawer sides, lacquer finish, 33 inches x 16 inches x 21 inches high. Photo by Bruce Miller.

these methods can represent the beginning and/or the end of the drawing process. In craft, because the designer and maker are one and the same person, decisions about incorporating new technologies are not driven by the evolved standards of the field and in turn by the demands of the professional marketplace; there are no standards to speak of, and not much of a marketplace, for that matter. Unlike the design fields, there is no organized network of firms hiring graduates of craft programs. Since craft is an essentially individual endeavor, craftspeople must apply the same creativity found in their work to developing a successful career path. Despite the obvious cost in terms of relative economic security, this results in a great deal of autonomy, including the freedom to decide what, when, and how new technologies are incorporated. Today's craftsperson might reasonably decide that digital technology provides no current benefit in the work, and, unlike a counterpart in industrial design, do so with no apparent harm to their career. However, will that individual want to, or even be wise to, make that same decision two, five, or ten years from now?

The late Peter Dormer, a respected author and journalist, said that almost nothing that is important about craft can be put into words and propositions. He wrote: "Craft is a body of knowledge with a complex variety of values, and this knowledge is expanded and its values demonstrated and tested, not through language, but through practice. It makes craft difficult to write about or even talk about with clarity and coherence." (Dormer 1997) David Pye has written about craft in ways that are useful. Pye favored the word "workmanship." He said that workmanship is the application of technique to making. "If design is what, for practical purposes, can be conveyed in words and by drawing, then workmanship is what, for practical purposes, cannot." Craftsmanship, he says, is "workmanship using any kind of technique or apparatus, in which the quality of the result is not predetermined, but depends on the judgment, dexterity, and care which the maker exercises as he or she works. …The essential idea is that the quality of the result is continually at risk during the process of making." Pye called this "the workmanship of risk." (Pye 1968)

That place in us where judgment, dexterity, and care converge in an act of making is where the spirit of craft lives and breathes. It is where the body and the tool, the material and the maker, join together; where the intellect, the emotions, and the senses all come into play. It is about body knowledge, a concept any dancer, athlete, or musician readily understands. And, it is about material sensibility. Craft is a dialog between the designer/artist, maker, tool, and material. In craft the creative practice is inseparable from the physical process of making, and so the making of an object contributes not only to the making of future objects, but also to their conceptual basis. I recently asked John McQueen, the renowned fiber artist, how closely his process of conceptualization was linked to his physical process of making. He said that they were inseparable, that he was always "thinking with his hands." This can be called "tacit knowledge," a term coined by British sociologists while studying scientific laboratories. They learned that regardless of how detailed is the written description of an experiment, it is only after scientists visit the lab where the successful experiment originally took place that they can duplicate the results. This tacit knowledge, acquired through experience, enables a person to do things as distinct from talking or writing about them. It is practical know-how, and is learned through interaction with people who already possess it. So, the craft classroom seeks to embed in the psyche the personal know-how of making, the tacit knowledge. By deeply ingraining the intimate and dynamic relationship between workmanship and design, it becomes a sensibility as much as a set of skills. This informs the process by which one evolves a vision for the work. This is the personal knowledge that will master the information found in any

Cupboard by Rich Tannen, maple bleached and dyed with lacquer finish, 44 inches x 16 inches x 12 inches. Photo by Bruce Miller.

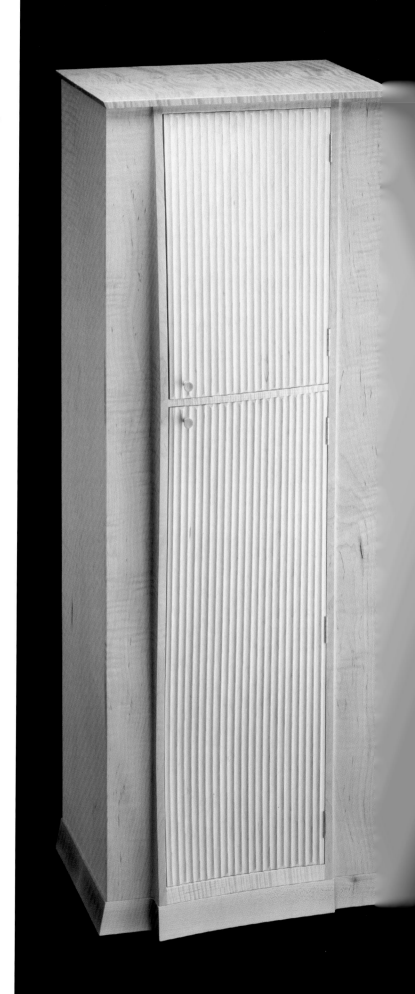

computer software. It allows us to embrace new technology and use it in inspired and constructive ways. This, as much as anything else, defines a craftsperson in today's world.

Many of the distinctions that formerly differentiated craft from industrial design and manufacture have become blurred. Hand-made vs. machine-made, one-off vs. limited edition vs. mass-production, highly regulated vs. rough, no longer have the same relevance. Today, designing and making exist along a spectrum of values, goals, and resulting work that no longer has clearly defined divisions. The power of the technology becomes transformative in this fluid and seamless interaction between CADD and CAM.

I have experienced this in my own work with these technologies, and found it both exhilarating and troubling. My ability to play with the technology, just as I might play with a carving gouge, in a kind of collaborative visual investigation of what is possible, was firmly grounded in my craft experience. The technology informed me with its potential, as I informed it with my experience. I attempted to tap into what it uniquely has to offer: in this case, the ability to take a complex surface of my design and describe it mathematically, so that the software could then interpolate the incremental cross-sections of that surface. The software can then, with a little help from me, describe that surface to a machine, which can, in turn, cut as many of those cross-sections as I ask it to, with whatever cutter profile I choose. I found this quite remarkable, and my hope was to integrate my craft sensibility and goals for the work with what the technology had to offer.

One could argue that CADD/CAM technology is driven by the desire to eliminate risk and is therefore antithetical to the notion of craft. Well, my shop is full of machines, and I use them every chance I get. On one of the pieces shown here, a chest for which I used CADD/CAM to create side panels, I also built two drawers. I cut the dovetails on those drawers by hand, not because of some romantic notion about the value of handwork,

but because that was the most direct way for me to achieve the results that I desired. I had little concern about hand-made as opposed to machine-made. This decision evolved directly out of my experience and my familiarity with the available array of technologies, and my choice of which best served my vision.

As exciting as the experience of employing the digital technology was, I also experienced a troubling isolation from the material and the act of making. I was intensely focused and involved during the CADD design, the designing of the tool-paths, and during the setup of the CNC (Computer Numerical Control) machine and its software interface. But, as I passively stood there watching our machine cut the parts, I felt very ambivalent about the role this technology was going to play for me in the future. I felt removed from the physical act of making.

The technology has reinvented the economies of scale in manufacturing in ways that could address some of my concerns. Automakers have succeeded in producing cars in quantities previously thought impossibly small. CADD/CAM technology inverts traditional thinking about distributed systems of manufacture, assembly lines, inventory, prototyping, and design development. Industrial manufacturing facilities have never had more opportunity to look and act like small craft studios, and vice versa. A craftsperson might actually own the means of production, the CNC machines. Or, businesses with sophisticated CNC equipment can cut parts in quantities small enough to approach one-of-a-kind. Subcontracting the CNC-cut parts, and focusing my efforts on the other components, could be an option. Then, at what point along the way do I cease to be a maker? At what point does my craft knowledge begin to erode, or become less important to my vision in the first place?

This technology is becoming more accessible to the small studio, and it is impacting many aspects of the work. As the craft studio acquires the potential to look more like the manufacturer, the economic

*If the crafts are to survive, craftspeople must survive,
and digital technology might play a role in helping make
a career in the crafts more economically viable.*

implications are obvious, and this is no small issue. Craftspeople trying to make a living from their work often have a hard time. These are people with a passion for what they do, and the limits of that dedication and commitment are tested at the margins of financial solvency. The economic relevance of craft to our culture disappeared long ago, but the relevance of economics to today's craftsperson is just as important as it ever was. If the crafts are to survive, craftspeople must survive, and I believe digital technology might play a role in helping make a career in the crafts more economically viable.

Digital technology can be a powerful tool in the hands of individuals with strong craft knowledge and a strong vision for the work that evolves from it. The problems break down into two principle concerns. First, the technology is powerful enough to erode and undermine those core values that give craft its meaning and relevance. The technology has embedded in its own design structure a kind of knowledge that can impose itself on the user and supersede or make irrelevant the knowledge of the user. Decisions made to incorporate CADD and/or CAM in a spirit of experimentation and openness to new ideas and market demands could, over time, have serious consequences. This leads to the second concern, that if craft is to remain viable, we must identify those qualities that give it value and take care not to discard them in our embrace of new technology.

Old and new technologies can coexist and create a healthy dialog that informs the work and challenges its meaning in ways that keep it fresh and relevant. Hand tools and CNC routers can complement one another in the hands, literally or figuratively, of a wise maker and/or designer. I believe that wisdom comes from in-depth core experiences, chief among them being the use of hand tools. This is not because I think all good craft must have hand work in it, although I believe a great deal of it inevitably does. It has everything to do with the values instilled through the experience, the fundamental principles

inherent in the process. Hand tools are at the heart of so many of the qualities that define a craftsperson's sensibility: they embody the values of judgment, dexterity and care. Through their use material comes alive, the development of body knowledge begins, and an intimate relationship begins between the understanding of a medium and the process of designing and making. This informs one's ability to think in all media, not just the one being learned.

Craft knowledge survives only through its practitioners. In a culture dominated by distributed systems of manufacture, uniformity, and consumerism, we must take care that this personal know-how continues to exist, and is manifested in the wonder of making. Though the crafts are marginalized today in almost every conceivable way, I believe they have never been more important to our culture, both in process and product, as an expression of important values that are at risk.

Further Reading

Edward S. Cooke Jr., *New American Furniture* (Boston: Museum of Fine Arts, 1989).

Laurie D. Olin, *Transforming the Commonplace, Selections from Laurie Olin's sketchbooks* (Harvard University Graduate School of Design. Brooke Hodge, editor, 1996).

Peter Dormer, *The Culture of Craft* (Manchester, U.K.: Manchester University Press, 1997).

David Pye, *The Nature and Art of Workmanship* (Bethel: Cambium Press, 1968).

Christopher Csikszentmihalyi, "Tacit Knowledge, Flickering Lasers, and Sweaty Tango," *Digital Dialogues: Technology and the Hand. A Studio-Based Symposium* (Deer Isle, ME: Haystack Mountain School of Crafts, 2004).

Wall Cabinet by School for American Crafts student
Jason Henderson as a senior in the BFA program,
cherry with lacquer finish, 36 inches x 9 inches x 6 inches.

Training the hand at the dawn of the digital age

To define the classroom, I'll begin with Ned Cooke's words in his 1989 "New American Furniture" exhibition catalog essay: "We aspire to train furniture makers who have mastered material and techniques as a means to explore design, content and imagery within the parameters of functional furniture. We are committed to the primacy of design and the use of appropriate methods and materials." In 1989 the range of educational experience considered appropriate to address those goals was contained within a reasonably identifiable and agreed-upon spectrum of options. Digital technology has changed that, and my experiences suggest that this technology has the potential to contribute to the vision for the work created in that classroom. However blurred the distinctions between art, design, and craft may have become, one value all of our students share is that they want to be makers, and so I am concerned as much with the process of designing and making as I am with the finished results.

Curricular decisions will evolve from our initiative in addressing these questions. They must take into consideration forces at work in the greater field. And, they must evolve from a clear vision of the core values that define the classroom. Those values must, in turn, be responsive to and weighed against evolving cultural changes, and at the same time hope to influence them. Whether the classroom is a college woodshop, a computer lab, or an apprentice's bench in a professional maker's studio, the values instilled and nurtured there become the prism through which we filter new opportunities and experiences and give them meaning.

What are some defining values of the classroom in which I teach? We are defined by the convergence of designing and making in one individual. I want to avoid the semantic questions of whether our students are craftspeople or craft artists, or artists, or furniture makers. The distinctions have all become blurred. I'm teaching at an institution that actually has the word "craft" in its name, an increasingly rare phenomenon today. Probably in our culture most people associate that word with the vendor displays they see in the aisles of the local mall, or the store in the plaza that sells colored twine and ribbons and candle-making supplies.

The craft-based classroom must make an unwavering commitment, not to learning the tools of digital technology, but to developing the foundation for using them wisely. We must develop a deep-seated understanding of, and familiarity with, fundamental principles and core values. In any curriculum, when new educational experiences are deemed important enough for inclusion, room must be made through the elimination of existing experiences. We must take care to retain those "traditional" experiences that are essential to instilling and nurturing core values and underlying principles in the first place, or they may be diluted and disappear over time. The dynamic relationship between the educational goals of the classroom and this technology is not always clear or apparent and can be quite insidious.

Can the traditional technologies of craft be integrated with the new technologies of CADD/CAM in the same classroom, without compromising one, the other, or both? The varying goals of today's furniture classrooms will address this question and will experiment toward satisfactory solutions to the delicate balance. At one end of the spectrum is the design classroom where no experience in making is deemed important. At the other end is the crafts classroom where making and designing are considered inseparable parts of the whole. Current and future artists/designers/makers will engage in the dynamic process of sorting out where along this spectrum they most comfortably exist. Nonetheless, core values must be at the heart of our classroom, and they must encompass the conceptual depth and understanding of design, so that all become inextricably linked in the process of making. Today's classroom must train a craftsperson who is able to adapt, to change, and not be bound by romantic ideals.

—*Rich Tannen*

Digital dreams, nuts and bolts

The digital camera (or the desktop scanner combined with film photography) is an excellent tool for developing ideas, as Amy Forsyth and Gabriel Romeu demonstrate here.

Forsyth, professor of architecture at Lehigh University in Pennsylvania, explains: "I had started to build this table, and put it aside for a while. When I came back to it, I couldn't decide what to do next, so I took photos of it, printed them out, and tried three different options by hand-drawing with color pencil on the print. I finally built the one on the far right, more or less." The table as built is shown in the photo at top right.

Gabriel Romeu, a full-time furniture maker living in Allentown, NJ, relies on computer-aided drawing for the glass and metal furniture he makes with his partner, Janet Richard. Romeu explains, "I use CAD for three major reasons. First is to conceptualize and proportion—a rendered drawing is quite useful for this, but so are wire-frame drawings and simple shaded drawings. From these, I can generate a shop drawing dimensioned directly by the software and including all the calculations for setting up stops, indexing tables, etc. The third is to generate CAM drawings (CAD drawings converted to code) that I mill with my Bridgeport CNC machine. A rendered drawing for presentation to a client is only a minor use of CAD, I would just as soon do that with a pen and paper. The advantage of CAD over conventional drawing is, it does things that are not within the capabilities of the pen."

top: Heartbreak Table
by Amy Forsyth, 17 inches x 18 inches x 15 inches, walnut, milk-painted mahogany, found wheel and mason's rake, 2004.

left and on page 1: 3-Tier Cocktail Table
by Romeu-Richard Furniture, 48 inches dia. x 17 inches, aluminum, etched glass, powdercoat finish. From the collection of Dean Thomas.

The advantages of digital manufacturing

CADD: *Computer-Aided Design and Drafting*

CAM: *Computer-Aided Manufacturing*

CNC: *Computer Numerical Control*

For the furniture artist, computer-aided design and manufacturing offers a number of valuable benefits. A very similar list of benefits would have arisen with the introduction of such powered machinery as table saws and band saws, early in the twentieth century, along with similar warnings about what might be lost. The benefits include:

- accurate cutting and shaping of parts in wood, soft metals such as aluminum, and plastic.

- efficient and cost-effective batch manufacturing of identical parts.

- the creation of shapes, surfaces and textures that traditional tools and techniques either could not practically make, or could not make at all.

Here are some examples of studio furniture designed and manufactured using computer-aided technologies. These pieces were exhibited together in a show called "Pioneering the Craft: CNC Technology in the Creation of Furniture," during The Furniture Society's 2004 conference in Savannah, GA.

Dialogue No. 1 two-sided chair by Matthew Harding of Canberra, Australia, hoop-pine and plywood, 35 inches x 35 inches x 33 inches, 2004.

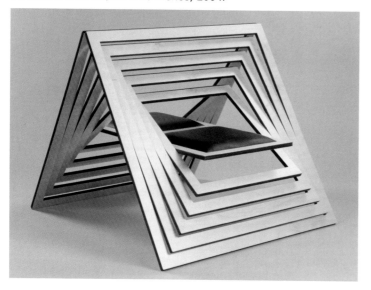

20/20 Standing Screen by Matthew Harding of Canberra, Australia, MDF and jarrah veneer, 92 inches x 40 inches x 10 inches, 2003.

Writes Harding, "Laser cutting and CNC router technology were key to the production of these pieces. The programs I write are not sophisticated and are designed to perform actions that the laser cutter likes to follow— simple geometry, repetitious elements with simple scaling, minimal non-cutting distance, and little material wastage."

Barcelona Bench by Peter Danko of York, PA, ply-bent maple, 35 inches x 72 inches x 22.5 inches, 2001.

Danko writes, "The all-wood bench is CNC-cut except the arm, which is bandsawn. The big parts could not realistically be cut any other way besides CNC, in this case using a three-axis Komo machine. The taper on the front edge of the side panels is made by cutting along a single curved 2-dimensional plane to a curved cross-section. To my way of thinking, it's subtle details like this that both express and take advantage of the CNC process."

Side Chair by Edward Wohl of Ridgeway, WI, cherry, 36 inches x 19 inches x 24 inches, 2003.

All the slats were cybernetically machined to the same shape (below). Wohl also digitized and CNC-machined the shape of the chair frame. He hand-sands the assembled parts to their smoothly flowing finished state.

Writes Wohl, "Since I have been utilizing a subcontractor to do my CNC work for 15 years, I have become more and more aware of the possibilities of production work. Even when designing one-off pieces I make patterns that could be used for multiples. I work very slowly and spend a great deal of time on tiny details."

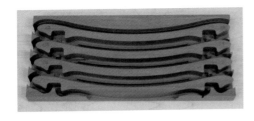

New Chips Off Old Blocks

Furniture professors choose their best student work

by Dennis FitzGerald

The learning process for a person who wants to make studio furniture, as in most specialized endeavors, is a roadmap with many choices on the way to the intended goal. While all of our experiences contribute to our learning process, it is possible with studio furniture to isolate three primary routes: self-taught, apprenticeship, and classroom. The following pages feature the work of young makers in a classroom environment.

When we asked the instructors to nominate their best students, we also asked for a description of the assignment and an evaluation of the results. We limited submissions to work produced in college-level classes of at least twelve weeks' duration, and to only one submission per instructor.

The furniture on these pages represents students at various levels of their educations, from a variety of programs. Included are beginners and graduate students, and work from programs specializing in studio furniture, product design, industrial design, architecture, craft, and fine art. It is furniture absent the rigors of professionalism and the demands of clients, where process and intent can be freely explored, and individuals have the opportunity to define themselves and their work under the guidance of professional faculty.

Dennis FitzGerald is coordinator of the woodworking and furniture program at the State University of New York, Purchase College, and a past president of The Furniture Society. The furniture shown in this story was on display during June 2005 at The Furniture Society's San Diego conference.

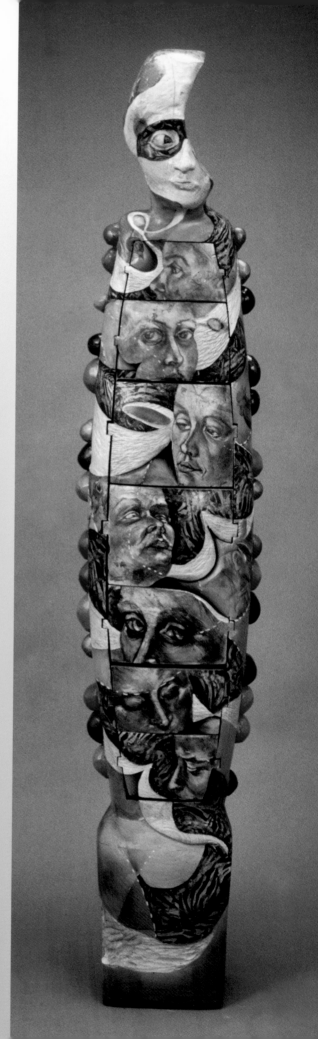

Untitled (see-saw chaise)
Kate Elliot, State University of New York / Purchase
Bending ply, veneer
86 in. x 18.25 in. x 24.5 in.
2004

Kate's piece, which she chose not to title, is the last of a series of works she has done that explores kinetic forms and also addresses the body. This particular piece functions both as a seesaw and a type of chaise. What I like is its sense of whimsy. One can see both a peapod and a mouth in its outline, and adding color to the edge accentuated those references. Its non-specificity as an object allows the sitter to approach it in a variety of ways: supine, astride, seated as on a bench, etc.

—*Michael Puryear, instructor*

left: Totem Pole
Elizabeth Alexander, University of Massachusetts / Dartmouth
Pine, pigment, tissue paper
68 in. x 12 in. x 9 in.
2004

The challenge presented to Elizabeth Alexander in this piece was to explore the nuances of personal narrative combined with sculptural form and the utility of furniture. The essential challenge…was to depict moods and dreams, the interior life of a woman, while integrating functional elements as a part of the overall concept. This was one of six projects which carried out the goal of her MFA thesis proposal. Her thesis works were dedicated to making both functional and non-functional sculptural objects imbued with personal narrative and imagery. In terms of originality, expression and craft, Elizabeth deserves special praise.

—*Stephen Whittlesey, instructor*

End Table Crank Box
Isaac Arms, University of Wisconsin/Madison
Douglas fir, maple, mahogany, steel
27 in. x 14 in. x 14 in.
2004

This is part of a series of pieces by Isaac Arms
that use cranks connected to rack-and-pinion
gear mechanisms to create movement. Turning
the crank causes the core to rise up and reveal
two drawers. The mechanical system includes
a metal counterweight that offsets the weight
of the drawer unit and makes the quality of
the action very smooth and solid-feeling.
The accompanying sounds are satisfyingly
mechanical and serve to spark the viewer/user's
curiosity about what is going on inside the box.
The action is irresistible—very few people are
able to stop cranking after one cycle. This is an
understated piece in terms of design style and
visual presentation, but it required complex
and meticulous execution behind the scenes
to maintain its conceptual integrity and
intimate quality.

—*Thomas Loeser, instructor*

Untitled (wall shelf)
Joe Lindeberg
Minneapolis College of Art and Design
Medium-density fiberboard, birch dowel, paint
50 in. x 30 in. x 10 in.
2004

The assignment: painted table, chair or storage
unit. An excellent shelf. First glance would raise
the question of how did the maker get the steel
stake through the cement block and the half-inch
plate steel? One needs to rap a knuckle on a few
parts to reveal that things aren't as they seem, for
the entire piece is constructed of MDF and two
birch dowels, skillfully faux-painted and textured
to appear as something else. This assignment
was executed with convincing success.

—*Dan Cramer, instructor*

Nomad Portable Bench
Brody Neill
Rhode Island School of Design
Carbon fiber, aluminum
2004

The *Nomad Portable Bench* seat is Brody's direct response to the nomadic lifestyle developing in the western world. An intelligent design relating to the demands of a shifting population, coupled with an investigation into appropriate material usage, has resulted in an elegantly designed and produced piece of furniture. The thin, wave-like form of the carbon fiber seat floats delicately on the scissor-action cast-aluminum legs, touching the ground lightly. Easily assembled and disassembled, the legs fit neatly into the underside of the seat and then the entire unit slips into a surfboard-style bench bag for easy transport. The assembled bench weighs less than five pounds.

—Peter Walker, instructor

Hall Table
Ryan Pfrommer
Herron School of Art (Indianapolis, IN)
Bent lamination, rock
34 in. x 42 in. x 13.5 in.
2004

This was a hall table assignment. This student went above and beyond his comfort range and built a piece that balances the weight of the trapped rock with the delicate nature of the bent laminations and supported table surface. The work employed new techniques for the student—bent lamination, setting a stone into a three-dimensional space—and was done with a professional level of craftsmanship.

—Cory Robinson, instructor

Torch Column
Kerry Krempasky
Indiana University of Pennsylvania
(Indiana, PA)
Cherry
24 in. x 6 in.
2004

…an excellent example of a class project featuring the synthesis of turning and furniture-related processes. Her piece incorporated both faceplate and spindle turning processes along with mortise-and-tenon construction, scroll-saw cutting, and spokeshave tooling. Kerry developed her original idea using several two and three-dimensional design processes featured in class, combined with her independent research of related artistic forms and concepts. Although this was Kerry's first woodworking and design course, she quickly developed her skills of technical understanding, process control, and craftsmanship during the formative stages of the project involving experimental turning and joinery construction, full-scale prototype, and model building.

Her decision to use only one wood (cherry) helped to visually unify the piece, allowing more attention to focus on the overall form. The dynamic effect of the cut-away regions complimented the linear contour of the piece as well. Kerry's sense of proportion and scale also contributed to the effect of the design, resulting in a continual movement of line and space. Her combination of turning and furniture-related construction processes were effective in achieving a structurally sound and well-designed piece.

—*Chris Weiland, instructor*

Extending Dining Table
Andrew Thompson
College of the Redwoods
Fort Bragg, CA
Pearwood, moabi
30 in. x 64 in. x 34 in.
2004

Andrew's goals for himself were to create an expanding table that was easy to use, and to work with veneers on a large surface. His concerns were that a single person could change the length and that the leaf be stored in the table. Refining a proven solution of the butterfly leaf with custom-made hardware, he was successful in executing a mechanism that operates smoothly without need for the user to be running all around the table. His selection of veneers for the table top yielded a pattern that looks attractive with and without having the leaf in place. The table is elegant in its simplicity, meeting his technical goals while providing a fine example of quiet craft work.
—*Michael Burns, instructor*

Book Box
Jennifer Jew
College of the Redwoods, Fort Bragg, CA
Pear, holly, Port Orford cedar
14.5 in. x 19 in. x 11 in.
2004

The case is built rectangular, full one-inch thickness stock, with blind, mitered dovetail joints. The final curved and tapered shape was achieved with hand tools, as was the cove-and-bead work. Drawer construction and fit is precise. Wood selection, details and finish are coherent and careful. Structural and decorative elements are successfully unified, as are simplicity and intricacy.

The grounded and calm appearance is what first grabs your attention. Up close, the builder's hand and intent is tangibly present in all details, big and small, from outlines and profile to surfaces, edges and reveals. An intangible and emotional appeal prevails. There is much here to discover. This box will find its right person, because it will define its owner. That's often how it goes with a box worth keeping.

—Ejler Horst-Westh, instructor

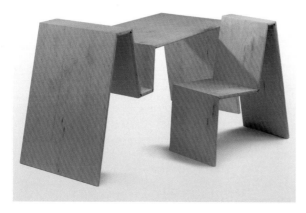

Desk and Chair
Douglas Williams
Milwaukee Institute of Art and Design
Appleply with maple veneer
56.5 in. x 25.5 in. x 33 in.
2004

The reduction of the design for a desk and chair set to essentially a linear problem enabled numerous alternatives in folded paper to be quickly produced and evaluated. The best of these were then refined using full-scale cardboard models. This process, along with Doug's sensibilities, led to forms which I see as original, well-proportioned, and eminently suited to the material. The inclusion of the rolled-under edge reduces the apparent weight of the pieces while making them visually more inviting.

Regarding the physical success of the pieces, Doug's tests revealed that epoxy-soaked joinery had similar structural properties as the rest of the material and that overall deflection would be the same, end-for-end, in the furniture as it was in the original Appleply sheet. The pieces therefore have the structural integrity necessary to be sat upon, danced upon, etc.

—*Stephen Lacey, instructor*

Transforming Tansu
Ben Kawaichi
College of the Redwoods, Fort Bragg, CA
Mahogany, madrone
37 in. x 32 in. x 17 in.
2004

The functional aspect of the kaidan tansu was a source of admiration for Ben's project. He liked the idea that this type of tansu also serves as a stairway. Ben believes that furniture is interactive in some way, why not make that interaction dramatic and playful? A series of attempts to arrive at a solution began with a Ferris wheel contraption that rotated containers through an opening. Ben realized that a simple form required a simple solution. He didn't want a gimmick that overpowered the function of the tansu.

The idea of having some mystery to his piece led Ben to conceal mechanics as much as possible. The tansu serves a purpose in its static state and reveals more as the user engages with it. Ben was successful in creating a well-made tansu true to its original function while attracting much fascination with its mechanics.

—*Greg Smith, instructor*

Lounge Chair
Jessica Lertvilai, Sheridan College, Toronto
Walnut veneer, laminated plywood
34 in. x 22 in. x 24 in.
2004

...a response to an assignment that explores the linear nature of furniture (i.e. stick furniture). Students investigate concepts of triangulation, compression, and tension, and develop a piece that resolves these considerations in a piece of functional furniture of a type of their choosing.

Jessica chose to focus on designing and making a lounge chair using a combination of bent-laminated and joined solid-wood elements. The linear nature of the chair frame, rendered in oiled walnut, contrasts effectively with the white-lacquered, pierced plane of the seat, made from bent-laminated poplar. Jessica's piece probes her interest in mid-century Modernism while demonstrating a high level of craftsmanship and exhibiting the potential for small-scale batch production.

—*Peter Fleming, instructor*

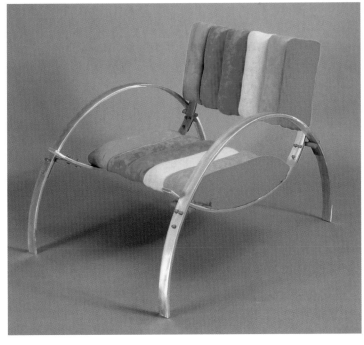

Untitled
Christy Oates
Minneapolis College of Art & Design
Aluminum, steel, foam, fabric
28 in. x 28 in. x 38 in.
2004

This is a wonderful piece for an introductory class in furniture design. Christy had a clear initial idea of what she wanted out of this project, solved a lot of construction problems along the way, and ended up with a chair that a person cannot just walk by without noticing. Upholstery is normally not introduced until later in the furniture sequence, so a piece like this is uncommon for a beginning class. When she said she had done some sewing before, I gave her the go-ahead for the proposal. This is a comfortable chair to sit in, with a smile.

—*Brad Jirka, instructor*

below, right: Untitled
George Mahoney
Minneapolis College of Art & Design
Carbon fiber, epoxy, steel
2004

This piece was part of an ongoing graduate series exploring and using carbon fiber composites. George worked out a successful hard-foam form, into which he laid the carbon composite material. This was built up and made smooth. Then the piece was upholstered with industrial-grade felt for a casual appearance. The base was constructed of high-carbon steel, all hardened and spray painted. The combination of a somewhat flexible composite seat and a somewhat flexible frame gives this chair's occupant a very comfortable sit. The felt invites the user to stay a bit longer.

—*Kinji Akagawa, instructor*

below: Stools
Dan Michalik
Rhode Island School of Design
Cork
20 in. x 16 in. x 14 in.
2004

Dan Michalik's cork chaise (not shown) and stools were the result of a year-long exploration of cork as a sustainable material with properties well-suited to furniture applications. After numerous prototypes and tests, Dan produced flexible stools that move with the subtle movements of the body. Laminating the cork with cuts in specific directions allows the movement and comfort of these pieces. Cork is relatively inexpensive, ages beautifully, and is sustainable. These properties were important to Dan in his efforts to create furniture that is produced with ecological sensitivity, aesthetic sophistication, and moderate cost. These pieces succeed on all counts.

—*Rosanne Somerson, instructor*

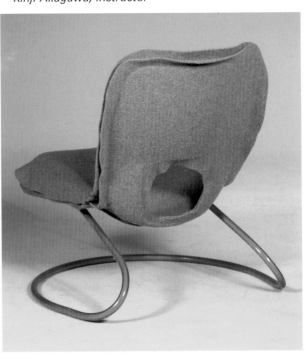

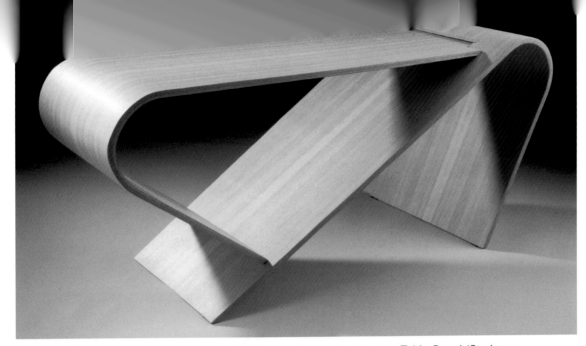

above: Ambiguous Table-Bench/Sculpture
Malcolm Majer
Rhode Island School of Design
Elm veneer
34 in. x 14.25 in. x 15.5 in.
2004

Malcolm's piece is one of the most successful projects to come out of last year's junior studio. The design brief stipulated the design and fabrication of two curvilinear pieces, bent-laminated or of plywood, that in some way relate to or depend upon each other. His project combines two identical elm veneer forms in a minimal yet conceptually sophisticated solution. The thoughtfulness with which the material is handled is balanced by a simple, ingenious approach to joinery and structure. Though obviously a furniture form, neither scale, material, nor structure lend it a clear identity. A pleasingly ambiguous presence suggests multiple interpretations, sculptural and functional.

—*Don Miller, instructor*

above: Table
Wes McGee
Georgia Institute of Technology
Baltic birch, CNC technology
16 in. 24 in. x 60 in.
2004

The intent of the project was to explore forms usually associated with bent laminate but executed in a novel method by utilizing the CNC equipment at GIT's Advanced Wood Products Laboratory. The project was created by stacking and gluing the same profile thirty-four times, then sculpting it into its final form. This form was created after an analysis of sixty different side and top profile variations, intersected using a constant cross-section. The resulting profiles were efficiently cut with a three-axis router from two sheets of 18 mm Baltic birch plywood. The assembled form was then sculpted on a five-axis router. Baltic birch was the chosen material because it sands to an extremely smooth surface. The table was constructed from three different sections of the profile, fifty-four total pieces cut from two 4 x 8 sheets. The finished product exceeded expectations with a very nicely styled and finished piece of contemporary furniture. Wes McGee, through this project, has become quite expert in the manipulation of three- and five-axis router technology as it relates to furniture design, form, and craftsmanship.

—*Alan Harp, instructor*

Iya Coffee Table
Brooke Davis, Purdue University
Walnut, glass, CNC technology
16 in. x 16 in. x 74 in.
2004

The coffee table has interesting technical and philosophical content. The form was developed in sketches, playing with the thought of being pulled in multiple directions at the same time. This tension can be seen in the twisting form of the table top, also emphasized by the subtle balance of the legs, especially the contrast of the large end leg with the smaller interior legs. Technically the piece has a number of interesting points. First, it was manufactured with CNC full 3-D production. This allowed subtle surface twisting and tapering. Second, the glass insert was made of water-jet-cut glass that has been bonded together to make the final form. It was also sandblasted to give a translucent appearance. Finally, the beautiful lacquer finish shows the beauty of the walnut grain.

—*Steve Visser, instructor*

Untitled (chaise lounge)
Kevin Veiths
Minneapolis College of Art and Design
Foam, epoxy
36 in. x 21 in. x 74 in.
2004

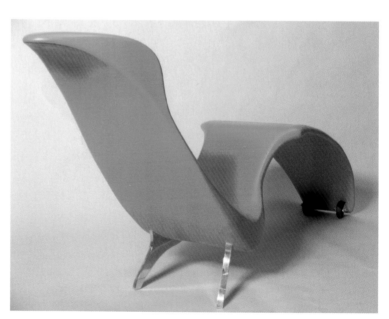

Kevin started this piece by gluing 2-inch profiled foam sections together, then shaping them to a smooth surface, followed by layers of glass cloth and fairing compound. The entire piece, when finish-sanded, was sprayed with a gelcoat for its final surface.

Kevin did an excellent job, both in his craftsmanship and his ergonomic considerations. A bit of playfulness is also exhibited by the use of urethane rollerblade wheels, which actually are functional because of the flex of the chaise when a person sits in it. This was a challenging six-week project, with goals that Kevin very successfully met.

—*Dean Wilson, instructor*

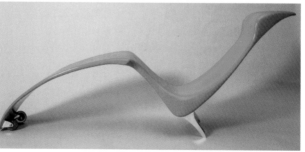

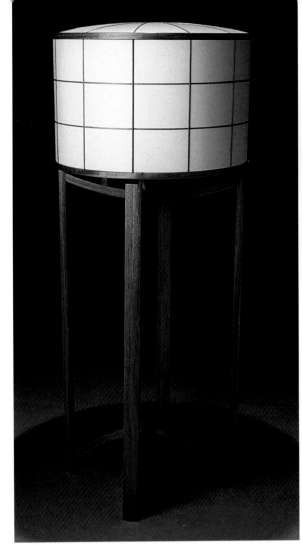

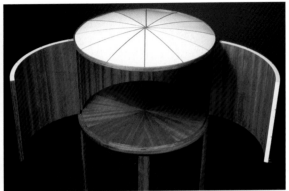

White Cabinet
Jefferson Shallenberger
College of the Redwoods, Fort Bragg, CA
Holly, bubinga
47 in. x 19 in. x 19 in.
2004

While careful work is the norm at College of the Redwoods, true innovation, as in any field, is exceptional. Jefferson has demonstrated his ability to work cleanly, quickly, and creatively. The *White Cabinet* is a good example of the result of his skills. His initial intent was to create a feeling of anonymity. Investigation is required of an individual to discover the doors, which are hinged and centered on grid lines.

Jefferson also wanted to combine calmness with motion. Drawing from Japanese architecture, the regularity of the grid gives a sense of repose while the pinwheel-like junction of the section lines of the top and floating effect of the suspended cabinet provide tension and a sense of potential activity. Though this is a technically difficult piece, its warmth is inviting.

—*Jim Budlong, instructor*

Chess Table and Pieces
George Dubinsky
Bucks County (PA) Community College
Mahogany, milk paint
31 in. x 34 in. x 34 in.
2004

Most of the chess pieces are turned, some are multi-axis turned forms. The size of the table and its height was determined by the chess set. The table and set were both well-designed and crafted pieces that more than fulfilled the requirements of the assignment. The table base is very organic, complex, and well-crafted. The set and table work well together. This work exceeded my expectations not only because George was a first-year student, but also because of how much he pushed himself in the design and technical areas to achieve such a great result.

—*Mark Sfirri, instructor*

Outdoor Bench
Jared Kay
Rochester (NY) Institute of Technology
Cherry, aluminum, Paralam,
interior eggshell glaze
60 in. x 14 in. x 18 in.
2004

The project encouraged students to investigate seating for multiple individuals while adding a secondary use. Our hope is that students will take a close look at the interactive qualities associated with furniture and study the connections of particular furniture archetypes as they relate to form and function. Most challenging was the balance of formal and functional—trying not to create a Frankenstein, but instead, fluidity in design and a piece that enables function to work in harmony with idea. In Jared's piece, the integration of storage was a good match for the chosen bench form. Jared also did an excellent job of researching and selecting appropriate materials that proved to be good aesthetic as well as practical solutions for a piece that could be placed outdoors. The components work well together and in both scale and character provide strong formal relationships and secondary levels of detailing. One criticism is that the form does not read as a bench but rather more as a hope chest. This results in the primary function not being very clear in terms of usability.

—*Rich Tannen, instructor*

Morning Jazz
Susan Link
Haywood (NC) Community College
Cherry, maple, veneer
54 in. x 40 in. x 10 in.
2004

If it were not for the Furniture Society conference in Philadelphia, Susan might not have considered this piece. Her knowledge of carving techniques has been enhanced by the more complex box form. The use of molded plywood for the compound-curved door presented other problems to resolve, i.e. hinging, fitting the door to an asymmetrical cabinet. Discovering the possibility of enhancing the door through veneer patterns takes it a lot further than the traditional book-match pattern she had originally proposed.

The inspiration from Wharton Esherick and Cubism is exciting since she did not literally translate Esherick forms or strict Cubist principles into a derivative design. The juxtaposition of the angled mirror to the twisted cabinet takes the dissimilar forms and marries them into one. The discovery in the interior of the cabinet of the corner of the mirror really completes this union of frame to box.

Morning Jazz won Best in Show in the Design Emphasis competition at the 2004 International Woodworking Fair (IWF).

—*Wayne Raab, instructor*

The Commission:
A Collaborative Process

by Jonathan Benson

Inlaid Dining Table
David J. Marks, Santa Rosa, CA
Quilted maple, ebony, wenge
31 in. x 48 in. x 72 in. to 108 in., 1994.

More of Marks' work is shown on page 37.

The client adds an important dimension to the creative process. While one might imagine that a maker would enter into this relationship purely for monetary reasons, many makers greatly appreciate their personal interactions with clients, as well as the creative exchange that can enliven their collaboration. The enjoyment of this relationship is also one of the main reasons clients will come back to a particular maker. To show just how the process works, here are interviews with five different furniture makers who do extensive commission work. Their approaches to the client-maker relationship vary as much as does the style of their work, though some common threads do flow through them all.

Established makers such as these five, with many years of being planted in their locales, have many pieces of furniture in use in homes and offices. Their work and their abilities are known. As a result, clients are likely to give them a great deal of creative freedom, once the basic objectives of a piece have been agreed upon and satisfied. Indeed, a degree of creative freedom is the key to a good experience for both maker and client.

These makers all report a basic two-meeting commissioning process, one meeting held in the environment where the furniture will reside, and the other often taking place at the workshop. When distance makes face-to-face meetings difficult, they can communicate via fax or the Internet, using websites to have a telephone conversation with both parties looking through the maker's on-line portfolio.

These makers tend to encourage a wide-ranging conversation, in order to understand a client's tastes in life and art as well as what Jack Larimore calls the "essence of an object's use, its relevance to their lives." Along the way they discuss function, scale, materials, finishes, schedules, and costs. But the most important part of these conversations may be what goes unsaid, between the lines, as maker and client establish personal rapport—in a sense, decide whether they like one another and will enjoy working together.

After the first meeting, the maker prepares several sketches to help the client choose a direction. These usually lead to more detailed drawings, a deposit, and then construction can begin.

Here's my own approach

by Jonathan Benson

My own furniture style is unique, and I am grateful that my clients have given me a lot of leeway in designing pieces. I feel fortunate for this freedom and try to reward that trust by giving as much of myself to each project as I can. This usually means starting with a new concept and making an entirely new set of jigs for most commissions.

I recall a client who has purchased several pieces from me. She initially purchased a wall-hung sideboard from my booth at a craft show and later wanted to commission a dining table to go in the same room. The original sideboard was titled *Samovar,* and was inspired by the painting of that name done by the Futurist Kasimir Malevich in 1913. I have found that the overall aesthetic of his work is at least as important as function, dimensions, materials, and colors.

After agreement on a set of working sketches, in most cases, my clients leave the rest the details to me. This allows me some of the spontaneity that motivates me in creative process. I design as I work, always making improvements along the way. No one has ever come back to ask why I didn't follow the drawings exactly. But often I do hear, as was the case in this example, "This is even better than I imagined."

Jon Benson of Hyde Park, NY, made two presentations on marketing at The Furniture Society's 2004 conference in Savannah, GA.

below: Samovar Wall Shelf,
Jonathan Benson, Hyde Park, NY
Holly, Swiss pear, curly maple
28 in. x 54 in. x 12 in.
Photo by James Hart.

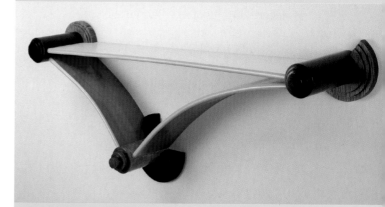

Coffee Table
**Boykin Pearce Associates,
Denver, CO
American walnut,
60 in. x 25 in. x 18 in.,
Photo by Jim Stayton.**

Boykin Pearce Associates, Denver, CO

The partnership between Tom Pearce and Dave Boykin has evolved over the past twenty years. After sharing adjoining shop space, machinery, and sometimes an employee for ten years, they decided to join together as Boykin Pearce Associates. As they pooled their resources, they developed a tight, high-quality experience for their clients. The two partners now spend all of their time in the office, with clients, or at the computer designing, and they employ three highly skilled craftsmen on the shop floor. Their work falls in between traditional and contemporary, with a simple and sleekly elegant look that belies the tremendous effort put into each piece. They frequently collaborate with other craftsmen who work in stone, metal and glass. Their clientele includes both residential and commercial customers: roughly 50% are homeowners and 50% are designers and architects.

The collaboration between these two maker-designers is never quite complete until the customer enters the process. They do virtually all of their work through the commissioning process, and the relationships that they develop with their clients are what truly motivate them. "Some clients even derive a great amount of glee from challenging us to go farther in some technical, aesthetic, or conceptual direction than we have in the past," the partners said—a challenge that is eagerly taken up.

After one of them holds a first meeting with the client, Boykin and Pearce meet together for a brainstorming session of their own, to create what they call the "story line behind the piece." Now the drawing can be finished, presented to the client, and final details worked out, such as woods, colors, finishes, and costs. What results from this process is "more than a piece of wooden furniture, but the tangible result of the relationship between maker and client: a collaboration of design, function, material, and the process of the client-maker relationship."

Billiard Table, Jeff Anderson of Boykin Pearce Associates. Felt and slate, 2001. Photo by Ron Ruscio.

Scarab Chair,
Wenge, eastern maple, fossilized walrus ivory,
24 in. x 24 in. x 37.5 in. tall, 1992

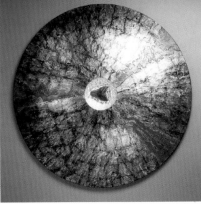

left: Alchemist's Disk #2
Cenozoic shark's tooth, patina
on silver leaf and copper,
5 in. x 45 in. dia., 1996.

below: Sitting Bench
Cast bronze with patina,
21 in. x 26 in. x 11 in., 1999.

David J. Marks, Santa Rosa, CA

David J. Marks started out in the 1970s making burl topped tables and clocks, and selling them at craft shows and stores in Northern California. Realizing that he needed to improve his skills, Marks worked for various cabinet and furniture-making shops, learning on the job. He then began doing antique restoration, and started making studio furniture and sculpture of his own design. Since 1981 he has shown his work in galleries, at exhibitions, and through numerous publications. He has taught and published extensively, his work has won many awards, and he is the host of a television program titled "Wood Works" on the DIY network that offers step-by-step instructions for building furniture that he has designed. Marks has also become very interested in patination, in which he combines painting, gilding (metal leafing), chemical patinas, and various lacquering techniques.

Roughly 50 percent of Marks's work is done on a commission basis. He finds that the maker-client relationship motivates him to "go off in a different direction that [he] hadn't thought of yet." Although the level of client participation varies greatly, he says most clients appreciate his creative force and allow him great latitude.

Marks prefers to have the second meeting at the client's home or office where the piece is to be placed. He brings sketches, a full-sized cardboard mock-up, extra cardboard and tape, and a knife. Seeing the space first-hand, Marks can quickly tell whether the piece will fit. If not, he can cut down the mock-up or enlarge it right there.

Jack Larimore, Philadelphia, PA

Jack Larimore's highly sculptural furniture includes tables, cabinets and chairs—and his sculpture is often based on furniture. Larimore looks at furniture-making as an exploration of many issues including, but not limited to, the use of a particular object and the essence of the daily ritual that occurs when using it. A table may be built for a particular function, but what else about the maker's and the client's life experiences can be gleaned from it?

Most people who are familiar with Larimore's work know that they probably won't get furniture that resembles anything they've seen before. A typical commission starts out with a far-ranging conversation that may cover such issues as why the clients want a particular piece, how and why they'll use it, what are their tastes, and what are their views about life and art. Larimore tries to draw out the essence of an object's use to determine its relevance

Long Port Bar, bubinga and lacewood, 10 ft. long x 7 ft. wide x 42 in. high, 2000.

Can the piece make a statement about the experience of using it, or about the environment in which it is placed? What can the piece do to become alive, not merely an object that happens to match the other objects in the room? Can it perhaps make a new statement about those objects?

To Larimore, everything is in the interaction with his clients and the process that evolves from that relationship and completes the idea. He does not see the finished piece as a reward for his effort; instead he strives to learn and grow from the commissioning process, the concepts related to living with his work, and the aesthetic exploration that results. The learning, growth, and pure fun resulting from this process are his reasons for doing what he does.

in the lives of its users. Although he does a tremendous amount of repeat business with clients who are accustomed to his wide-ranging approach, new clients do have to adjust. Typically the part of the conversation that concerns the physical attributes of the piece is limited to dimensions and such functional concerns as the need for a drawer or the size of the top. Says Larimore, "Once the essence of the piece is established, the physical attributes follow."

Larimore's clients give him a lot of leeway, so the design takes shape in the studio as the piece is being built. He says, "I feel lucky to be connected with people who engage in this process and appreciate the result. I feel that this process makes me a better designer, keeps me in touch with the larger world outside my studio, and gives relevance to what I spend most of my life doing."

Wishbone III
Cherry and leather,
41 in. x 25 in. x 40 in.

Larry and Nancy Buechley, Chamisal, NM

Larry and Nancy Buechley have been working together since 1975, when they set up a shop in a beautiful hidden mountain valley. They were both art majors in college and had focused on painting and sculpture. Upon discovering the process of bent lamination, they were able to translate their love of the creative process into furniture design. They maintain an equal partnership, sharing all of the design and construction responsibilities. Each has strengths that play off the other. They put an equal amount into the creative process as well. One or the other comes up with an idea in the sketchbook, then they bounce ideas back and forth before finalizing the design together. Sometimes the process involves putting the idea aside to let it develop in the subconscious. This is possible because they usually have several projects going on at any given time. Once agreement is reached, construction begins, but ideas continue to evolve during the building process while they work together in the studio.

Roughly 50 percent of their work is done on commission, often based on pieces clients have seen in galleries, shows, or the homes of friends. They also do a lot of repeat business, with many clients wanting to continue a theme started in an earlier piece. The Buechleys see their job as a "juggling act between the stylistic inclinations of form and the function that the client needs to fill." In general, "clients determine the function of the piece, then they leave us a lot of aesthetic space." Clients come to the Buechleys for two primary reasons: first, they like the style of bent laminations, organic curves, and natural materials, and second, they can't find anything in the market to fulfill a functional need. "People are different shapes and sizes," Larry says, "and the commissioning process resembles the tailoring of a suit." The Buechleys always strive to achieve a simple and clean solution to the original challenge. "These simple, clean solutions take a lot of effort," they note.

Kerry Vesper, Scottsdale, AZ

Kerry Vesper's work combines stack-laminated plywood with fine domestic and imported woods to create sculptural and often organic forms. His work ranges from the functional, such as tables and chairs, to the moderately functional, such as his beautiful non-turned bowls, to nonfunctional sculpture. Vesper has been working with wood since the 1970s. With only one full-time helper, he feels that he can only produce a limited amount of work. He sells through galleries, high-end craft shows, and word of mouth contacts. He estimates that only 30 to 40 percent of his work is done on a commission basis, but he enjoys the process and would like to do more. Though mostly residential, his commissions have included four church-related projects.

Vesper's style is unusual, but he has been able to find clients who want that particular vision. He is very open to client ideas that can fit into his way of working. During the first meeting, he tries to judge how much input the client wishes to have. He also attempts to judge how well his clients will be able to visualize what the completed project might look like. He finds that "the more involved that the client is, the more they feel that it is their piece." He enjoys this input and believes that it is an important part of the process. Occasionally a collector wants a piece that was made by him and won't be concerned about its function or design details, a freedom Vesper savors.

Once the function and overall dimensions of the piece have been established, Vesper usually works up three ideas to present in the form of sketches, a Styrofoam mock-up, or a clay model, depending on how much visual help the client needs.

Vesper says he often "tells clients that their choice of what they buy is just as much a creative statement as the artist's work." He obviously enjoys working with clients who are involved in the creative process. "It is exciting, but also scary because I have to have the time and the ability to produce what I said I would."

Altar, for Lord of Life Lutheran Church, Sun City West, AZ.
Sapele, Baltic birch, wenge
30 in. x 53 in. x 20 in.

Table and Chair
Baltic birch and cherry,
29 in. x 30 in. x 30 in. (base),
with top 60 inches diameter.

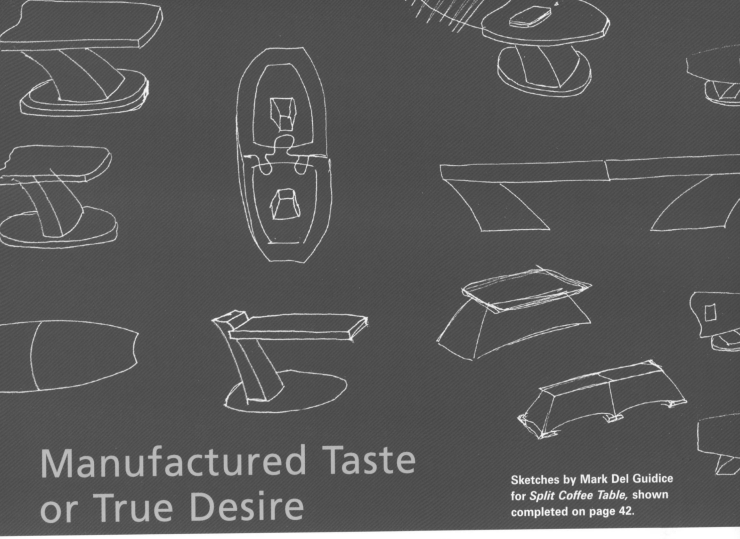

Manufactured Taste or True Desire

Sketches by Mark Del Guidice for *Split Coffee Table*, shown completed on page 42.

How commission artists learn to 'read' the client

by Brooke Carnot

What is taste? Initially, the debate on "taste" revolved around beauty. In 1757, in his essay, *Of the Standard of Taste*, David Hume, the Scottish philosopher, wrote: "It is natural for us to seek a standard of taste; a rule, by which the various sentiments of men may be reconciled; at least, a decision, afforded, confirming one sentiment, and condemning another." He argues that beauty is in the eye of the beholder: "Beauty is no quality in things themselves: It exists merely in the mind which contemplates them; and each mind perceives a different beauty." (Hume 1757) And in *An Essay on Taste*, Baron de Montesquieu wrote:

> Poetry, painting, sculpture, architecture, music, dancing, the different kinds of games, and in a word the works of nature and art, can give [the soul] pleasure: let us see why, how, and when,

they give it; let us endeavour to account for our sensations: this may contribute to form the taste; which is nothing else but an ability of discovering, with delicacy and quickness, the degree of pleasure which every thing ought to give to man. (Montesquieu 1755)

Montesquieu suggests that the human mind innately possesses a notion of what is beautiful and that each individual uses his or her own senses to classify varying degrees of beauty in other things. Accordingly, beauty does not exist in everything; "beauty" is one of many conscripts of judgement— both positive and negative—and there are varying degrees of beauty.

Brooke Carnot is a London-based freelance writer with a graduate degree in social psychology from the London School of Economics.

An uncertain client, and one new to the commissioning process, requires a lot of hand-holding. For his *Split Coffee Table* (below), Mark Del Guidice began with a series of sketches (previous page), made an informal presentation drawing, and then built a small model (right). This piece netted Del Guidice the 2005 Niche Award in the Painted/Colored Furniture category.

In the hundred years that followed, "taste" had become a matter of much debate. Social theorists aimed to determine not only what was beautiful, but who decided. In his book *The Theory of the Leisure Class*, the American economist Thorstein Veblen argued that the wealthy were less concerned with the beauty of things than they were with the appearance of their consumption to others:

> The taste to which these effects of household adornment and tidiness appeal is a taste which has been formed under the selective guidance of a canon of propriety that demands just these evidences of wasted effort…If beauty or comfort is achieved… they must be achieved by means and methods that commend themselves to the great economic law of wasted effort. (Veblen 1899)

In fact, for Veblen, beauty was not the goal, but rather a natural byproduct of the conspicuous consumption of "food, clothing, dwelling and furniture." Beauty, therefore, is immaterial; what is important is the witnessing of things between "friends and competitors." (Veblen 1899) It is at this point in social theory that the debate on taste centered around "keeping up with the Joneses." Theorists emphasized that taste is determined and policed by the wealthy as a method of determining one's status and rank.

Later in the twentieth century, in keeping with social theory that focused on the importance of the individual, Erving Goffman, a Canadian researcher, educator, and author further articulated a growing belief that aesthetic choices were a mode for communicating personal preferences; a symbolic, non-verbal code for the viewer to decipher. In *The Presentation of Self in Everyday Life* (1956), Goffman wrote: "The private office of an executive is certainly the front region where his status in an organization

is extensively expressed by means of the quality of his office furnishings."

What is "taste" in the twenty-first century and, more to the point, what is its effect on the studio furniture market? The theorists of old, while alluding to a socially constructed, symbolic consensus on beauty, did not have cable television and media conglomerates. Multi-media message-makers deliver a feast of form and color, dictating to those who watch and read what is available for consumption in ways that could not have been imagined in previous centuries. Mirja Kalvianen, a contemporary social psychologist who writes extensively about design, believes people are affected by television programs, magazines, and the home environments they experienced as children. But, she cautions, while magazines and television programs are prolific, only certain messages about style endure because they fit the society's general trends, lifestyles, economical situation or cultural rituals. David Linley, the noted English cabinetmaker, said, "Subliminally, of course, people are affected by trends and popular themes because the trends define what is on offer in the market as a whole. …The press will even hone in on items we have been producing for years—trends in interiors tend to be cyclical." Kalvianen argues that artists and designers are bound by their own internal codes and

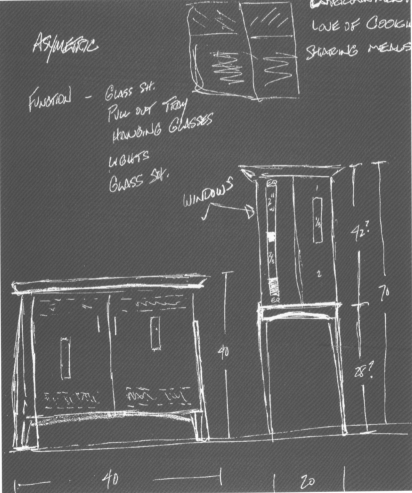

His-and-Her cabinets by Mark Del Guidice. When working for a couple, Mark Del Guidice found their requirements for one cabinet so incongruous that he proposed a pair of cabinets. The clients signed off on this sketch.

bindings that keep them from exploring too far beyond the norm. As Robert Frost said, "An idea is a feat of association." New aesthetic sense will draw on the history of furniture making as studio furniture-makers press the envelope. But a distinction still needs to be made between style and taste. Whereas style can be conveyed through the media, taste is personal. Kalvianen says that certain messages from the media "will stick when they fit your lifestyle." In other words, we are selective viewers, not automatons.

American studio furniture is rather young—traceable to the work of Wharton Esherick in the 1930s and his influence on subsequent makers, such as Sam Maloof and George Nakashima in the 1950s. Perhaps the co-emergence with mass media and mass markets is not a coincidence, but rather a healthy reaction. While hundreds of interior design magazines and dozens of programs may indicate the current furniture fashion, economic or personal reasons may draw people to mimic what they see. Esther Kaplan, a psychotherapist and seasoned buyer of studio furniture, points to a fear factor that helps perpetuate market trends in furniture: "It is a more comfortable zone to be like everyone else," she explains.

"Unique," "one-of-a-kind" and "one-off" are words that pervade the commissioning process. Mark Del Guidice, a furniture maker working in Boston, proffers, "If you stop and really think about what it is about a certain object that touches you, you'll more than likely find out about your own values and your experience. I like tapers because of buttresses in architecture that I was exposed to as a young person. They give strength to things." Like Montesquieu, Del Guidice wants to examine our personal system of sentiments—our personal "taste." Ric Allison, a furniture maker in Philadelphia, makes a valid point about economics and a domestic culture that constrain the purchasing of furniture: "People choose their own music, see live bands. Everyone around me and in my shop listens to something different. With music people feel they can change their tastes, an album is only twenty bucks. The furniture they

feel they will have to live with for the rest of their lives." Just as with music, it is individuation that drives commissions. Not only do certain people want their iPod stacked with songs that suit them, but also they want their living space to do the same. Furniture makers and buyers want something that is outside the commonplace, but how far outside is a matter for discussion. If the furniture maker were designing for himself he could imagine a piece of any kind and construct one that was at the very limit of his capabilities. However, the commissioning process is not entirely about him. It is about the desire of the client, and the maker must navigate that. For the process to work, maker and client must both dance a dynamic yet delicate tango.

From the perspective of the client, there is a spectrum of makers. At one end is the maker who characterizes himself as the engineer, and at the other end, the artist. The engineer produces a finished work with little modification of the design proposed by or agreed to with the buyer. The artist, on the other hand, may adhere to as little as the function requested (bed, table, chair) and instead sets off to make a piece that is his own creation. It is important to note here that artists in the field of studio furniture do not eschew technical skill, but embrace it. As well as drawing on inspiration and raw data, they employ methodological expertise.

From the perspective of the maker, there is also a spectrum of clients: at one end the client who trusts the process, and at the other, the client who cannot relinquish control because they have not enough trust. Three chief factors combine to affect the client's ability to trust: their knowledge of the maker's previous work, their own experience commissioning pieces, and their ability to trust the artistic process. The first two are easy to gauge, the third can often be measured in the initial interview. Makers admit that they can end a commission before it even begins, based on their initial impression of the client and whether it seems possible to work together.

David Linley offers clients what can certainly be called a service and a process. "I think of myself more as an engineer than an artist. I am not their

left: Longhorn Dining Room Table by Ric Allison.

right: Ric Allison began this table commission with a series of sketches made during and after a visit to the client's home. The longhorn theme was not specified by the client but rather emerged in Allison's drawings.

interior decorator, I am their maker." And as such, Linley (who studied with John Makepeace) would be found closer to one end of the spectrum. His clients are invited into a series of design steps. An initial discussion defines the client's request. Initial sketches are drawn. And only after the client agrees with the detailed brief will they proceed. A watercolor rendering of the design is painted to show scale, proportion, and color. Finally, a computer program is used to produce the technical drawing that will become the workshop blueprint. The client is consulted at every stage and is welcome to participate throughout. Says Linley, "The older I get, the more structured and risk-averse I become. I don't like seeing a table and the handles are on the wrong side or the drawers are too fat and the drawer sides are too thick. I want all that contained, so write it down! It is a matter of asking endless questions." Linley bears the weight of responsibility to get it right and his design process is testimony to that. But that is only one style of doing business.

Ric Allison, a master craftsman and established commissions designer, has a method that is altogether different. He builds a mental collage inspired by his visits to the house and with the client. He asks esoteric questions about what they like and what their habits are. The answers are not directly applied to a design but do inform it, along with the information his senses gathered and his subsequent musings on the client and their environment. There is no set manner in which a piece is finally achieved. He says:

I try not to give too much information in drawings, only impressions and general shapes…I find that if you give them too much information, too clear a picture, they want what you've drawn exactly. Well, I don't design this way. I refuse to build this way because it leaves the surprise out of the equation. …There is a chance for tearing the whole thing down at some point, reworking some small detail and illuminating some small part of it to make it a completely new piece, less static, more knowing, less easily categorized. As I grow older I see more and more the complexities and mismanaged delight in discrepancies. It is what makes us humans exciting.

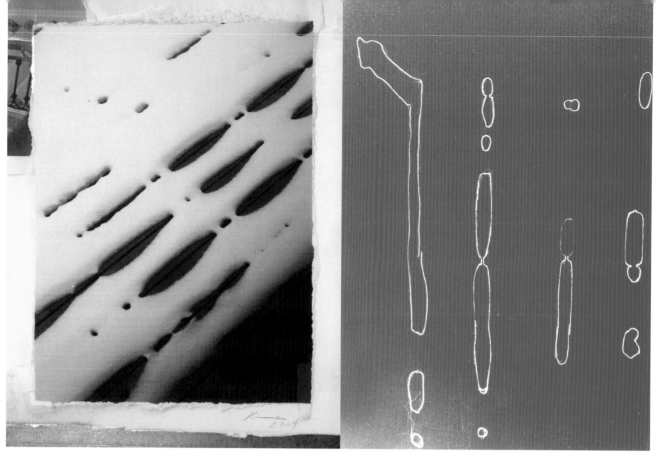

left: Allison's snapshot of snow melting on the client's deck. *right:* A drawing Allison traced from the photograph at left, allowing him to create and detail the credenza *(overleaf)*. These images led to the credenza door detail. Esther Kaplan, the client, had sufficient experience with the commissioning process to trust Allison, allowing him to create and detail the credenza without looking over his shoulder.

above: Credenza doors, with surface detail derived from the pattern of melting snow on the client's deck.

The vexing scenario is the client-couple who are unable to agree upon a shared design idea. Del Guidice had just such predicament and concluded that his-and-her cabinets were the solution to satisfy the aesthetic needs of both husband and wife. The ideal tango between maker and client, on the other hand, is exemplified in the relationship between Allison and his client Esther Kaplan, who commissioned him to make a credenza. On the spectrum of makers, Allison is toward the pure artists, though unquestionably a technical wizard and impeccable maker. He silently wends his way through his client's home, picking up insights about how they live, and more importantly to him, "what is missing" in their lives. He gleans information from the "hapless happenstance of mundane things in the corner of the room, the stack of laundry that sits neatly folded in the corner, the cracks in the snow on the deck that comes once a year from the snow melt, the particular smell of what was cooked an hour before you arrived." Allison's work assimilates the poetry of his client into a piece not only for them or about them, but about what he thinks is a part of them they have not yet realized. As the client, Kaplan expresses her knowledge and experience: from her custom-built house to its individual furnishings, nearly everything has been made to order. She learned of Allison through an art consultant/friend. She had seen his work and liked what she saw. But she said, "I let the artist do what they do best. I told Ric what my needs were, but I went to someone who has the imagination…and you know what? You hold your breath!" Kaplan trusts and the artist creates and

the piece is completed beyond her satisfaction. The Allison/Kaplan combination is rare. Typically, both the maker and client are somewhere closer to the middle of their respective spectrums. Under such conditions, the key to a harmonious completion is communication, communication, and more communication.

Credenza by Ric Allison, commissioned by Esther Kaplan.

In this era of service, a furniture "engineer" will be beloved by his client and his work will stand the test of time. But in an era dominated by mass markets and mass-production, the artist may do just the same while challenging the status quo in society and in the client. As Del Guidice says, "Some of us stay with safety and some take risks, which result in personal growth. We all love living on the edge, but we tend to stay with safety rather than overcome our fears. For those that know or sense the truths of life it is compelling to move forward. It takes courage and society recognizes this, and sometimes rewards it as well." ♟

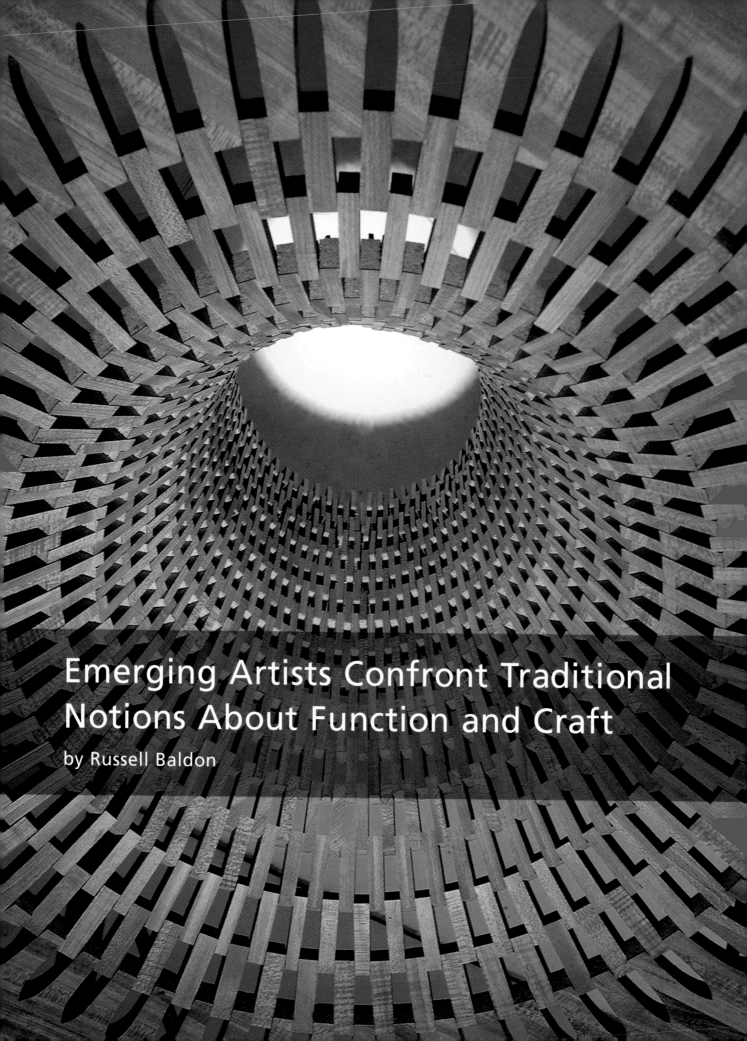

Emerging Artists Confront Traditional Notions About Function and Craft

by Russell Baldon

Here is work by twelve emerging artists. The pieces I have selected for this report, while expensive, rare, and intellectual, are to furniture what concept cars are to the auto industry: they provide questions, directions, and information about what we as a culture are thinking regarding the built space that surrounds us.

Many of these pieces do not function in a classic utilitarian sense, but they all strive for meaning using a visual language that we as viewers can readily understand. There has been criticism of this genre of furniture (a chair isn't a chair if you can't sit in it) but this ignores an important point: we interpret our world through the physical objects in it, based on more than their functionality. This expressive work confronts the traditional notions of function and craft. Work by these young makers has an edge or idea that sets it apart, as they explain in the notes accompanying their photographs.

Russ Baldon studied at California College of the Arts and Crafts and San Diego State University, and has been artist-in-residence at the Oregon School of Art and Craft. He makes furniture in Oakland, CA. In Furniture Studio 1: The Heart of the Functional Arts *(1999), Baldon selected and introduced a dozen young furniture makers in a provocative article titled "Next." We invited him to take a new look for his next dozen promising new makers, out of school and young in their careers.*

Scott Oliver, Oakland, CA

left, and far left: Loop
Plastic laminate, particleboard, steel legs and hardware, galvanized wire; 30 in. x 40 in. diameter; 2003.

Kitchen tables were my first sites for community—for socializing and being socialized. So for me all tables are locations for discourse and embody the rules of behavior I learned to engage in these interactions. Any table or other manmade object is to some degree the manifestation of a set of social values. The fake wood grain and particleboard table top in *Loop* brings into play its own set of ideas about mass-production, beauty, nature, and utility. Parsing the table's surface and reassembling it into the fabric-like, vortex form at the center of *Loop* heightens the artificiality of the materials and confounds their imminent disposability with a carefully crafted symbol of entropy. In treating the table top in this manner I make palpable the tension between the material world and the immateriality of the ideas that shape it.

Cory Robinson, Indianapolis, IN

From T-Town to the Back Acre
Poplar, charcoal drawing, graphite, paint
22 in. x 20 in. x 6 in.; 2003.

By exploring the varied impacts of gesture and line, my work functions between the specifics of place, the defining characteristics of gesture in the landscape, and the more generic qualities of line and mark-making as a way of activating the furniture form. My intent is to engage the viewer not with the practicality of use, but with an emotive response to the piece and the challenge of discovery in finding function for the work.

When choosing materials as a furniture-making medium, I utilize the practicality of wood but do not always rely on its inherent qualities as a source of inspiration. Some investigations do not rely on furniture-making process and craftsmanship alone to further the works, but instead use the impulsiveness and emotions that can be created within drawn and painted surfaces.

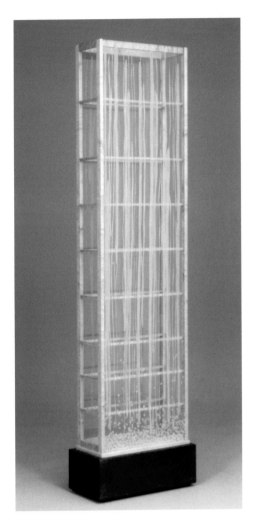

Kirby Jones, Portland, OR

Water Cabinet 1
Wood, glass, granite
70 in. x 10 in. x 20 in.; 2002.

Listen to the pulse of life, feel its rhythm, appreciate its wonders. There are syncopations in the order we all try to achieve and it is these deviations in the fabric of life that make it so vibrant and beautiful. It is amazing what can be heard coming from the background of the noise of our lives, but so often in the chaos of our hectic days we forget to look for it, to acknowledge, reach out, and embrace it. There are echoes and reverberations bouncing off the walls of routine, pointing out the need to look beyond and walk into the mystery. Connections that we take for granted can be found, and within the contrasting dualities commonly attributed to all manner of things, an intertwined core is revealed.

My recent work is about reflection—a tool with which to find and enjoy the magical simplicity of what's around me. At its foundations it is about a reverence to nature—asking the viewer/user to embrace what is around us and take a moment to think about what is essential and important in our worlds. It is an opportunity to reflect, to appreciate life, and to connect with the energy that ties and binds all things.

My work is personal and I feel an intrinsic link to it, seeing it not as a result of my ideas but as an extension of myself, as I do not believe in a separation between artist and art. It is spiritually charged and based on ideas that are spiritually important to me, yet I also strive to make my work universally approachable.

Simple and deliberately suggestive, my furniture's stylized naturalism is meant to connect the mind of humanity with the power of nature and offer a space in which this can be realized.

Sylvie Rosenthal, Penland, NC

40 Minutes or Less
Found, acquired, and salvaged wood;
92 in. x 18 in. x 19 in.; 2004.

This piece was very much about process, an exercise in building fast and on the fly, glue and screw and deciding as I went. I wanted a big mass, a big shape, something that felt solid and dense. This piece was built from one end to the other and really could have kept on going.

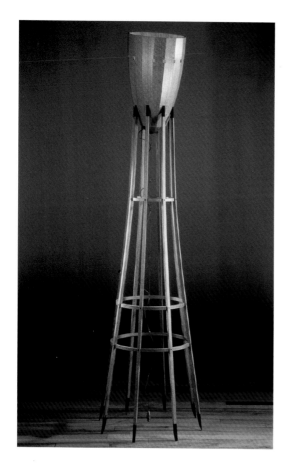

Nick Hollibaugh, Providence, RI

above: Wyola 2003
Copper, white oak, wenge
96 in. x 23 in. x 23 in.; 2003.

right: Night Stand
Maple, stainless steel, mahogany;
24 in. x 20 in. x 68 in.; 2002.

My work is primarily influenced by architecture.
I fell in love with the building process through
a series of carpentry jobs, along with art school
training; I found a happy medium in creating
furniture. The process of building different types
of structures is something I relate to very easily.
I moved to the East Coast about four years ago
and it made a big impact on the types of objects
I was creating. The ornate style of architecture
that dots the New England landscape was
very stimulating to me. Shingles, scales, and
clapboards have all found their way into my
work. These have combined with memories
of the barns, silos, water towers, and grain
elevators of the Midwest landscape in which
I grew up. New objects I create reflect the
patterns, complex structures, and natural patinas
found in these almost forgotten structures.

Allison McLennan, Oakland, CA

Laocoon
Plywood, Formica, wood, paint
60 in. x 60 in. x 12 in.; 2004.

This sideboard was inspired by an ancient Greek sculpture. It depicts a priest and his two sons entangled with a giant serpent from the sea. Currently, I am finishing up a second version that is the same design, but it is three-dimensional; the figures are carved out of foam and then covered in fiberglass. This series is a new direction in my work, a step into thinking in the round, and into thinking beyond the functional right-angles that furniture often involves.

left:
Ineinander 2002
Wood, steel
14 in. x 16 in. x 12 in.; 2002.

far left:
Ineinander 2 2003
Wood, steel, paint
120 in. x 18 in. x 16 in.; 2003.

below:
Hammock Bench
Wood, steel
32 in. x 55 in. x 20 in.; 2001.

Don Miller, Cranston, RI

Relationships with the world of objects continually advance and recede as our bodies navigate physical space. As we sense these interactions, patterns emerge that identify objects of use as extensions of the mechanical body. This fundamental identification underpins the concept of function.

The human body senses purpose on a level deeper than these specifics of use. Our perceptions of scale, spatial orientation, materiality, and manufacture are foundations for the identities that we project upon functional objects. My current work investigates the origins of this identification between the body and everyday objects.

On one hand, abstract forms draw specific meaning from their context. On the other, familiar forms, when abstracted, evoke the universal. Each view affords a vantage point from which to regard the interrelatedness of the subject and object. This dialectic of subject and object, of user and useful, is an essential way we manifest our world: as both experience and metaphor.

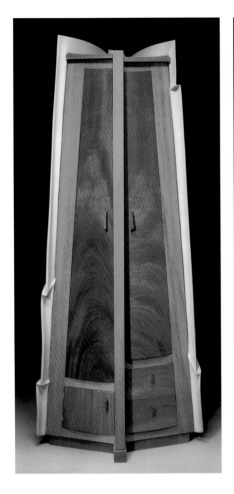 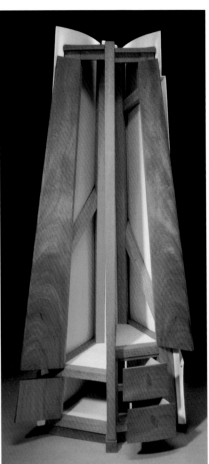 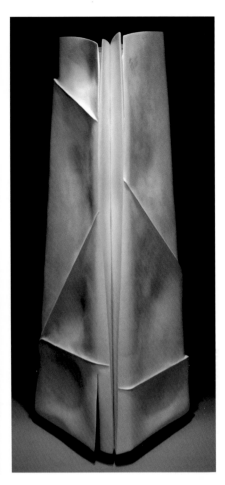

Gian-Paul Piane, Fairport, NY

Cabinet (left to right: closed, open, back)
Mahogany, poplar, varnish oil, milk paint
30 in. x 30 in. x 72 in.; 2003.

As I make a piece of furniture, I carefully and purposefully advance it towards a point where it becomes its own individual, no longer mine. I then become an observer, knowing full well that the object is now bigger than I am: it has extended beyond my idea, and I am now serving it instead of the reverse. I then fade into the rest of the world and the object becomes the subject of my admiration as it now holds a mystery that is greater than the sum of its parts or its process of creation.

I share my creative expression between the fields of architecture and studio furniture. It is as an architect that I have become aware of the influences that affect the process and outcome of creating an object. In architecture, the approach to realizing an idea is always a curious chemistry, a purposeful and temperamental composition of personalities, circumstances, and ideas. For me, this chemistry is a dynamic source of inspiration that manifests itself in the final object.

The awareness of these influences has helped me focus my work as a studio furniture maker. This focus is directed towards exploring the transcendental aspects of personal experiences. I use the imaginative mystery surrounding these experiences to create expressive pieces of furniture that embody the process involved in creating them and their source of inspiration. Sketches are my initial point of departure, from which the making process is steered through reaction to both material and emotion. These sources allow me to achieve a strong connection with the purpose of my work, and have enriched my process of making along with my experience of the final object.

This approach is a purposeful departure from the premeditated and calculated process of design that I am accustomed to in architecture. I find that it frees my creative exploration to possibilities and awareness that a "predetermined end" method would not allow.

Jason Schneider, San Diego, CA

His and Her Cabinets
White oak, cherry
20 in. x 46 in. x 14 in.; 2003.

I am interested in exploring the wonders of masculine and feminine psychology through functional cabinetry. Many of the concepts are based on common stereotypes as well as on direct and indirect experiences.

In *His and Her Cabinets* I explore masculine and feminine identity through the use of line, proportion, and material. Together the pieces support each other much like in a loving and caring relationship, but like many relationships that decide to go their separate ways, the cabinets split apart and are able to stand on their own (with the help of a hidden leg) until they potentially connect to another piece of furniture in the future.

Matthias Pliessnig, Providence, RI

top: Shell
Mahogany, cast concrete
26 in. x 16 in. x 73 in.; 2003.

above: Span
Ash, cast concrete
18 in. x 16 in. x 77 in.; 2003.

A bridge is a span from one point to another. This short definition encircles countless objects and ideas in our everyday world—a leaf stretching over a crack in the sidewalk, a bridge connecting two islands, or even the networks of our thoughts. By moving from state to state throughout my life, bridges have become a metaphorical object that continuously circles back in my work.

Creating *Shell* and *Span* simultaneously, I wanted to use different structural methods to achieve the connection of the foundations. The frame of a kayak with the bow of a bridge influenced the skeletal structure of *Span*. Danish cord was used to "skin" the skeletal structure, defining the form and allowing seating. *Shell* is a very thin form acquiring its strength from the geometry of the compound curve. The cast concrete bases act as foundations, as the earth would act to a bridge.

Barbara Holmes, Oakland, CA

above: Incorporated (installation), 2004–2005
Reclaimed hollow-core doors, fluorescent fixtures.
Afterhours (skyscraper), 52 in. x 15 in.
Smokestack, 18 in. x 18 in. x 120 in.
Afterhours (commercial park building),
60 in. x 24 in. x 16 in.

Hollow-core doors are often taken out of homes in the event of a remodel or demolition project, some find there way into resale shops, but most end up in the local landfill. In my current work I am reclaiming and reworking this dismissed, discarded, and valueless material. When cut up and assembled the once inane object begins to take on a new language of large-scale architecture and modernist structures, lending the work to the creation of installations and complete environments. In these works immediate visual relationships can be drawn: The interior material used to describe an exterior edifice, the part used to represent the whole, and ideas of use and reuse.

above: A Solution for Contention
Wood, stainless steel, mirror, soap, cotton cloth
59 in. x 28.5 in. x 13 in.; 2000.

There is a mixture of the nonsensical and serious when we encounter the superstition that "if two people wash in the same basin they will be bound to quarrel." In this piece, there is an attempt to take old ideas and notions about the nature of our world and bring them into a current context. *A Solution for Contention* is a washbasin and mirror that is absurdly split by a single line with soap and washcloths at either side. There is also the inclusion of scripture (*Genesis* 13: 8–9) on the inside of the mirror frame which talks about Lot and Abram dividing their land to keep peace between their herdsmen. Issues of separation, division, and the conflicts that often arise when lines are drawn become relevant to very personal spaces and to borders between nations at large. Here an arcane superstition takes on the vast topic of social conflict that spans human history.

Matt Hutton, Portland, ME

Core Sample
Wenge, plaster, army men, hair,
BBs, metal dust
10 in. x 10 in. x 25 in.; 2004.

*How concrete everything becomes
in the world of the spirit when an object,
a mere door, can give images of
hesitation, temptation, desire, security,
welcome and respect.*

Gaston Bachelard,
from *The Poetics of Space*—1958

There is an ambiguity to my work.
Virtually all my works are vaguely narrative
often using barriers or a dichotomy
to express the concepts within them.
Absurd functions and ideals become these
barriers at times, to manipulate the
audience's motions and concerns.
This creates a ponderous relationship
between the piece and its participant.

Furniture, architecture, and literature are
all strong influences, and this hybridization
results in peculiarly familiar forms. I offer
the possibility of a more meaningful and
desirable experience with a familiar object.
I use the cabinet form in many instances
due to its distinct division of interior and
exterior space. This austerity provokes
physical manipulation by the viewer/user.
With an emphasis or over-exaggeration
of physical motions such as the opening
and closing of doors, drawers, etc., I'm
able to invoke an intimate thought or
moment. This physical act is an aid
or tool used to enable a dialogue
between the viewer/user and the piece.

Alive and Kicking...

*but the business of making furniture
is no easier in England or Scandinavia*

story and captions by Bruce Burman

above: Small cabinet of cherry, about 15 inches in height,
is suspended with perfect stability in an outer frame by
a system of wedges. It is an outstanding example of the
ingenuity of the self-taught Swedish maker Dr. Hans Ahnlund.

Furniture designer-makers who,
like me, work on their own or
perhaps employ one or two others,
find it hard to make a reasonable
living. I was curious to know
how makers in the developed
economies of Scandinavia and the
U.S. succeeded, and in 2003 was
fortunate enough to be awarded a
Churchill Fellowship that enabled
me to investigate at first-hand. The
experience enables me to compare
how makers from Denmark,
Sweden, the United States and the
United Kingdom go about their
business. I am able to draw on data
from more than forty makers who
range from one just starting to
perhaps the most celebrated of all,
Sam Maloof.

To avoid later regretting a failure
to ask the right questions, I
produced an interview checklist
that contained sections dealing
with the business, its facilities,
financial data, order book, and
marketing. I took photographs of
workshops and furniture as well as
a portrait of each maker. Furniture
makers are creative people, usually
with a lot of character, and all
those I met were generous with
their time and hospitality.

A Void in Denmark

Despite all my efforts, and
with support from a Danish
businesswoman, I was unable
to identify a single designer-maker
in Denmark. I concluded that
several factors have led to their
demise, the preoccupation of the
Danes with the work of top
designers perhaps being the most
significant. There also seems to

be a fair amount of employment bureaucracy, and little support for small businesses.

My visit to PP Møbel, a company specializing in producing the designs of Hans Wegner, gave me a good insight into the way the furniture business has moved in Denmark. Most of their output is chairs produced with an intriguing mix of advanced machinery, high-quality materials, and hand-finishing. The end result is a quality product from an internationally known designer repeated consistently, which is important for a registered design. For the celebrated first televised U.S. presidential debate between Richard Nixon and John F. Kennedy, NBC purchased Hans Wegner-designed chairs made by PP Møbel. Not to find a single furniture designer-maker in Denmark was surprising, but Sweden, on the other hand, was quite different.

Swedish Hospitality

All the Swedes I met were very hospitable, going to great lengths to look after me and show me something of their beautiful country. Public transport there is a joy to use and so easy to plan journeys that I was able to do it all from my computer at home, right down to bus journeys from small provincial towns where no rail connections were possible. It is impossible to avoid comparisons with the shambolic state of our own transport system in the U.K., but the differences in other spheres are equally stark. For a start, the Swedes really do look fit and healthy. They dress well and look happy. I saw no loutish behavior, no booming stereos, and no litter. Surprising amounts of graffiti and quite a few beggars were evident in the major cities and served as a reminder that the Swedes have problem areas, too. What, you may ask, has this got to do with my study of furniture makers?

Well, it's my belief that the outward symbols of a country give clues to the national character of its people. The Swedes are very organized and take pride in what they do, and this is evident not only in the way they train cabinetmakers but also in how makers do business. The Carl Malmsten Center of Wood Technology and Design in Stockholm runs a three-year cabinetmakers' course that culminates in the students making a final piece graded by outside masters. On my visit, my namesake Leif Burman, who runs the course, showed me a final piece of such extraordinary quality that it left me feeling very humbled. No wonder there are five or more

Bruce Burman is a furniture-maker and journalist based in Exmouth, Devon, in southwestern England. Burman was awarded a prestigious Churchill Fellowship to finance his tour of furniture makers in Europe and America (he's shown at left receiving the award from the Duke of Kent). The oak sideboard, above, is an example of Burman's own work. An earlier version of this article appeared in three parts in the British magazine Furniture and Cabinetmaking.

left: The detail on the box lid is a fine example of the technique of raising grain as a form of decoration, developed by the innovative Swedish maker Dr. Hans Ahnlund. *middle:* This chest of drawers by David Lamb is an outstanding example of the quality of cabinetmaking in America. *right:* This rocking chair is by Gary Weeks, a very successful maker and astute businessman, who has skillfully exploited a niche market. Every mother-to-be in America needs a rocker.

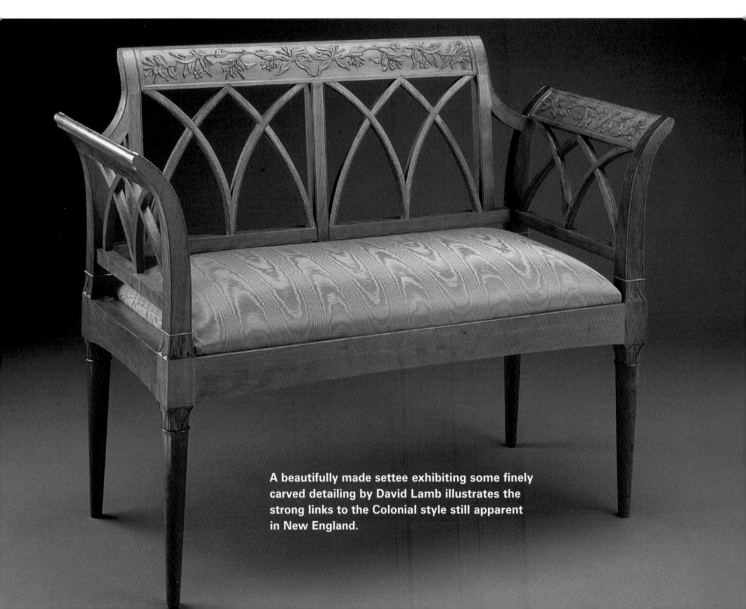

A beautifully made settee exhibiting some finely carved detailing by David Lamb illustrates the strong links to the Colonial style still apparent in New England.

left: Table by David Lamb. *right:* A sewing box by Per Brandstedt of Sweden is one example of the many small impulse items displayed in his showroom. Such an acquisition can lead the buyer back with a more substantial commission.

applicants for every place and only those who have already been employed in a workshop for at least a year will be considered. I doubt the limited high-quality training available in the U.K. is quite as rigorous as the Malmsten center in Stockholm. My only experience in the U.S. was the College of Redwoods in California, which failed to impress, not least because a two-year course included no insight into running a furniture-making business. Given this level of training, how do the Swedes fare in the harsh reality of the commercial world? One of the commercially most successful makers I met was in Sweden.

Another maker in Sweden, Dr. Hans Ahnlund, had no training when he left academia to make furniture. He was the most inventive maker I met and should provide encouragement for the many people who aspire to make furniture but have not had the time or resources to undertake formal training. The cabinet shown suspended in a frame by cunning wedges is but one example of his ingenuity. The cabinet was absolutely rock-solid in the frame.

Ahnlund told me of a discovery he had kept to himself for many years. When he had some particularly bad dents in a piece he was making, he tried to plane them away but soon realized they were too deep, so he resorted to moisture and heat. The effect was to raise the compressed fibers of the dents above the surface he had lowered by planing. He could see the potential for decoration in this technique, so he made a simple outline of a key with wire and used it to tap an impression into a piece of maple. He then tried to plane the impression away, as he had with the accidental dents, and finished up with a raised outline of the key. Ahnlund has since done much to refine the technique, as shown in the box on page 62.

I was not surprised to discover when I analyzed my findings that only two of seven Swedish makers I interviewed could be said to make a living from their business without the need to supplement from other activities, or from a partner's income. One of the two was earning a significant proportion of what was a very modest income from restoration work. In both cases, the makers were successful in a niche market.

left: Bowl by Per Brandstedt. *right:* Michael Creed's sense of fun is present in all his work; the two humidors in the center of the page are an example of how he manages to inject humor into what would normally be a prosaic item. *below:* This bookcase by Per Brandstedt demonstrates his business acumen. During lean times, components are made and stockpiled. Then when orders come they can quickly be satisfied, since the bookcase can be assembled and finished in about 16 hours.

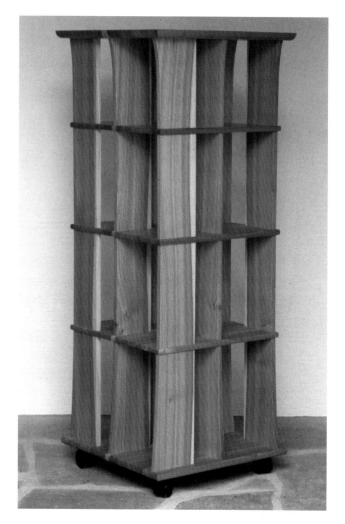

Awestruck in America

America strikes me as a land of extremes: size, climate, wealth, poverty, and achievement. Perhaps a measure of extremes can be seen in the furniture produced there. Certainly, in the U.S., I came across the finest work I saw on my travels, and the most commercially successful of all the makers I interviewed, but my impression was that there was not the same level of consistent quality to be found in the U.K. and Sweden.

The great diversity of peoples in the States makes it hard to discern national characteristics in the same way that it is possible in Sweden and the U.K., whose peoples grow up surrounded by visual reminders of their long cultural heritage. The diversity of cultures in the U.S., on the other hand, gives rise to a wide range of styles. That said, in New England I noticed how strong the bond is with the Colonial style and the Shaker tradition. Perhaps the finest craftsmanship I saw in the States was made by David Lamb, who lives within a mile or two of a Shaker community.

In my tiny sample, the proportion of makers in America earning a living from their business, without supplementing their income from another

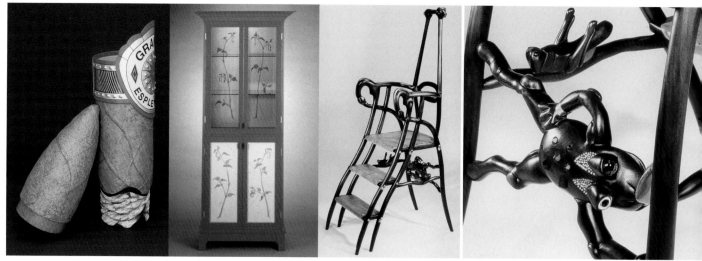

left: Humidor by Michael Creed. *middle:* Cabinet by Per Brandstedt. *right: Library Steps* by Michael Creed. This piece changed forever his ideas about the marketing value of exhibitions, when a delighted customer overpaid substantially for hurry-up Christmas delivery. *far right:* Detail of the library steps.

source, was seven out of twenty-three, a very similar proportion to Swedish makers. However, three of them were contributing to their revenues with such activities as paying apprenticeships, teaching, and writing. Three of the makers were successful in a niche market, and one of these was by far the most successful of any maker I interviewed, with annual revenues three times that of the most successful Swedish maker. I suspect the proportion of makers able to sustain a living exclusively from furniture making is very similar in the U.K.

Niche Marketing Succeeds

All the makers who had identified a product for a niche market found this a successful marketing strategy, and the two most successful makers were the best at exploiting this strategy. In most cases the making process had been refined and components were made in batches to be stockpiled. This worked well because components could be made at less busy times, take much less storage space than the finished article, and an order could be quickly satisfied. Gary Weeks, of Wimberley, TX, has been particularly successful at identifying a niche market and satisfying it with a well-made product, at a price that people will pay and that leaves a reasonable

profit. It seems that every mother-to-be in America wants a rocking chair, and his sell well, despite the competition. There are other factors at work, such as carefully targeted advertising, streamlining batch production, and setting up an excellent delivery system. And like his very successful Swedish counterpart Per Brandstedt, Weeks's wife plays a key role in the business. Brandstedt developed a bookcase so that he can make components for it during less busy times and put them together from stock when there is demand. He has orders for two bookcases for the Royal Palaces, so he must be doing something right.

Some makers had the space for a showroom, and exploited the advantage by making smaller items with a price that fell into what might be termed the bracket for impulse buying. Brandstedt, the most successful of the Swedish makers, had wall-mounted candle holders, simple little boxes, and a variety of smaller pieces to tempt clients once they were in his showroom. He found that even though such a customer might not commission a piece of furniture on the first visit, ownership of the smaller piece would often lead them back for a more substantial order. Makers know the value of getting

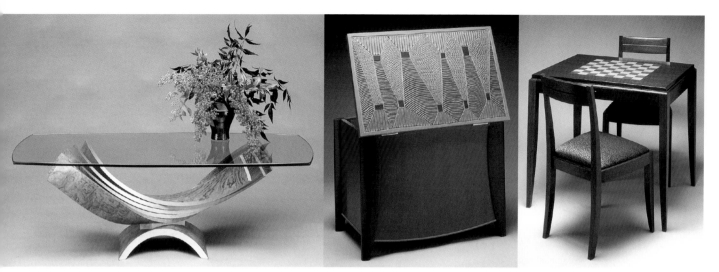

left: Blaise Gaston adopted a neat strategy for a reliable and economic delivery system by designing a series of coffee tables that when disassembled can be packed within the maximum UPS parcel dimensions. *middle: I See Fish...I See Ties Chest* by Michael Cullen, who is rare among designer-makers for totally separating the fees for designing and for making. *right: Games Table* by Michael Cullen.

a prospective client into a showroom or workshop, and Andrew Varah's workshop and studio in converted seventeenth-century barns in England are the ideal places to tempt a client.

Some makers use galleries to sell work, with varying success. A commission of around 40 percent on sales was fairly universal, and enough to turn a significant number of makers away from this source of business. Exhibitions were more widely used, but again with mixed results. Michael Creed of Lynchburg, VA, told me he spent several days at an exhibition where he had lots of inquiries but no sales, and vowed not to go through the experience ever again. Some time later he had an inquiry about the library steps he had exhibited, and when asked the price he made up a figure on the spur of the moment. He heard nothing for a while, and then the same person asked if he could deliver the steps in time for Christmas a few days later, a considerable distance from the workshop. The client was so pleased she added an extra $2000 to her check. Creed reviewed his ideas about exhibitions.

More Knotty Problems

A reliable method of delivering orders is particularly important, and nowhere more important than in America. Gary Weeks, the very successful maker with a product selling well in a niche market, needed a reliable and economical delivery system, and he has gone to considerable trouble to achieve one. This included developing a bulletproof and cost-effective method of packaging his rockers, and tracking them so that he can telephone the client when it arrives to be sure she is happy. As a way of reducing delivery costs, Blaise Gaston of Earlysville, VA, designed a beautiful glass-topped coffee table, which when disassembled fits into the UPS maximum parcel dimensions.

Almost all makers have to put up with inquiries that involve varying amounts of work but fail to materialize into a commission. When such inquiries involve some design work, most makers receive at best a notional compensation for their time. This negative aspect of business was most apparent in Sweden. Michael Cullen of Petaluma, CA, was one of a very small minority of makers who separated the design process from the making and charged a design fee, paid before any design work was done.

left: An elegant contemporary writing desk made of lacewood by Andrew Varah, a highly regarded and successful English designer-maker renowned for the versatility of his work. *right:* The wooden home of Swedish maker Per Brandstedt is at the end of a gravel path with a well-equipped workshop on the right and timber storage barns behind. Here Brandstedt has close to the perfect working conditions, a significant factor in his success.

The working environment can be a major contributor to the success of any designer-maker, and this view of Andrew Varah's house, studio, and workshop, built in 1653 in the heart of England, close to good rail and road links, is a fine example of an ideal setup.

left: Sideboard from the *Dramatic Stripe* series by husband-and-wife team Wales and Wales. *right:* This chest of drawers was made of English walnut and ripple sycamore by Andrew Lawton, an English maker whose work is becoming more widely recognized. Like many ecologically sensitive makers, he prefers to use British, European, and North American hardwoods from renewable sources.

In the unlikely event of the client not proceeding after the design stage, the client would be free to take the design to another maker. Those with the courage to adopt this strategy found it very successful at eliminating casual inquiries and did not think it turned anyone away.

During the period of my fellowship, many makers were finding that orders were hard to come by. Some had enough work to tide them over, while others adopted new strategies for keeping the wolf from the door. Bespoke kitchen work was one ready source of income for a number of makers, while restoration work appealed to others. In most cases this type of work paid as well as, if not better than making furniture. Those with a niche product or who had national reputations seemed less vulnerable to market changes. Some makers in America were in the enviable position of having their work collected, a practice more common there I suspect than in Scandinavia, or the U.K. for that matter.

All successful makers had their own Web sites, and found them useful as shop windows for their work. While no maker could estimate the amount of work generated through the Internet, all agreed that a Web site was essential. Many made use of collective

sites such as www.furnituresociety.org or www.guild.com. Nearly half the makers had no printed brochure and it may be that the Internet is supplanting this method of publicity.

The Swedish makers' cooperative, with its gallery in Stockholm, and the Furniture Society and New Hampshire Furniture Masters Association in America, are examples of organizations which actively promote the craft and sale of handmade furniture. Their contribution is significant. The Worshipful Company of Furniture Makers is the nearest U.K. equivalent to these organizations. While it promotes good design and high standards of making through the Guildmark awards, it has a long way to go before it can compare with the support for individual makers provided by those organizations I encountered in Sweden and America.

Great Workshops and Working Partners

Unsurprisingly, the most successful makers had close to the perfect working environment. The ingredients include a spacious workshop next to their home, often with a showroom, excellent machinery and tools, and no shortage of materials storage space. Per Brandstedt's premises were ideal

above: A walnut bookcase by Martin Grierson reflects his mastery of form and function, here combined in a harmonious and perfectly proportioned piece.

right: A Gentleman's Dressing Chest by Martin Grierson illustrates why the work of this much-admired English maker has received many prestigious awards. The more you study this exquisite piece, the more apparent is the subtlety of its detail and proportions.

but the only ones I saw in Sweden of real quality. In the U.S. I came across quite a few really good setups and concluded that the availability of land at relatively low prices must make it easier to create the ideal working environment. In the U.K., Andrew Varah's premises are a rather nice example, perfectly sited for easy travel for his clients.

In my study, the two most successful makers of all had partners actively involved in the business, looking after administration and marketing. These makers were also creative, energetic, and driven people with a well-developed business sense. In the U.K., Wales and Wales are the best example I know of a husband-and-wife team, both highly creative people involved in the making process. Surprisingly, the majority of successful makers I interviewed had not started their working lives

as furniture makers. This does not hold true for the six makers from England whose work is shown here.

A Glimpse of England

Although I have not had the opportunity to study makers in the U.K. with the same intensity that my Fellowship allowed me to do in America and Scandinavia, I do believe that there is something of a renaissance in the English handmade furniture business. Could it be that the buying public is at last recognizing that heirloom-quality furniture commissioned by them is a more satisfying alternative than antiques? A good barometer of the marketplace is the "Celebration of Craftsmanship and Design," an exhibition staged annually in Cheltenham. The exhibition has the work of some seventy makers on view and attracts significant

Cod's Eye chest of drawers made of elm and beech by Barnaby Scott of Waywood is a fine example of the very high-quality furniture produced by one of England's top designer-makers.

numbers of the buying public from far and wide, and the quality and variety of work is very impressive indeed. While John Makepeace and Alan Peters are internationally known, there are a number of makers whose work will stand comparison with the very best, and for this article I asked a representative cross-section of them to contribute. The work of Martin Grierson, Andrew Lawton, Barnaby Scott, Senior and Carmichael, Andrew Varah, and Wales and Wales illustrate the variety and superb quality of contemporary furniture to be found in England today. These examples speak for themselves. All of these highly talented and

successful makers have their own Web sites, which carry more details of themselves and their work.

The business of making handmade furniture is certainly alive and well in Scandinavia, America, and the U.K. The quality is as good as it has ever been, and there are signs that the wider buying public may be recognizing the wonderful opportunity there is to commission a beautiful piece of furniture. The Internet may be the catalyst needed for the buying public to see what is available, and to learn what is involved in the commissioning process.

below and right: Here is the much-acclaimed desk for the Marquis of Bath, designed and made by Senior and Carmichael to hold his personal collection of photographs.

left: Inspired by the Chrysler building, Andrew Varah made this eye-catching drinks cabinet, which incorporates an infinity model *(above)* and a perfect scale model of the building's elevator doors in its base. He is probably the only designer-maker to incorporate infinity models in his work.

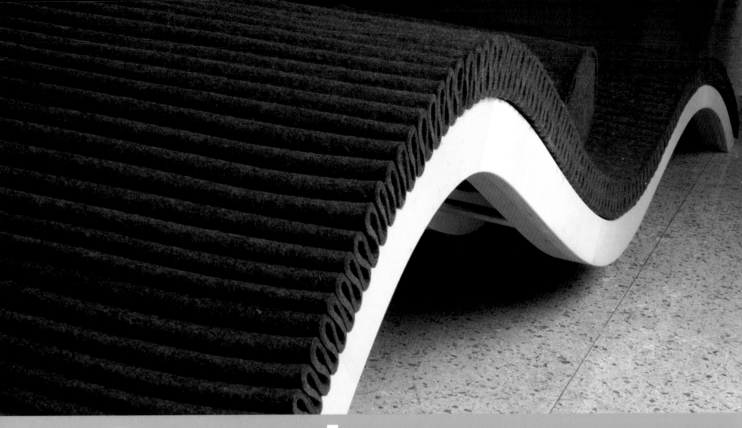

Curv-iture

A straight line is not always the shortest distance

essay by Suzanne Baizerman
photo captions by Oscar P. Fitzgerald

Dr. Suzanne Baizerman, associate curator of crafts and decorative arts at the Oakland Museum of California, wrote this commentary for the catalog accompanying The Furniture Society's "Curv-iture" exhibition. "Curv-iture" opened during the Society's June 2004 conference in Savannah, GA, before traveling to the Hickory (NC) Museum of Art, the Gallery of Art and Design at North Carolina State University in Raleigh, the Denver Airport Concourse A, the Houston Center for Contemporary Craft, and the Florida Craftsmen Gallery in St. Petersburg; for dates and details please visit www.furnituresociety.org. Jurors for the exhibition were Baizerman, Dr. Charlotte V. Brown of North Carolina State University, Dennis FitzGerald, Furniture Society past president, and Garry Knox Bennett of Oakland CA, a leading maker and 2004 recipient of the Society's prestigious Furnie award for lifetime achievement.

The exhibition title "Curv-iture" has served, as might be expected, as a potent stimulus to the latent Baroque tendencies of participating furniture makers. Or perhaps it stirs reminiscences of the decorative excesses and humorous tangents of the 1960s and 1970s. Whatever the explanation, "Curv-iture" is the freshest, liveliest furniture exhibition to appear in a long time. In the here-and-now, we can immerse ourselves in another world, one with curves, where few straight or angular lines are allowed. Many of the works pulse with vitality, contrasting with others where curves suggest repose.

Two of the more energized works are Kim Kelzer's *Vera* (p. 79) and Jill Henrietta Davis's *Palindrome Birthday Brocade Table,* (p. 74), both harking back to the pattern and decorative movement of the 1970s and its strong female presence. Kelzer's deliciously patterned table virtually pirouettes on slender legs, its feet *en pointe*. Davis's table strikes you with its brocaded glass tablecloth fluttering in a breeze. Not to suggest that it is no surprise that the makers of these pieces are female, but there is an implicit femininity, delicacy, and in the case of the glass table, fragility. Other lively touches in the exhibition are the deep undulations of David Hurwitz's aptly titled *Blue Taffy Mirror* (p. 75) and the animated anthropomorphic lamp, *Benny Goodman,* by Cosmo A. Barbaro (p. 74).

Counterpoints to these pulsing, energy-raising pieces are the quieter, contained works emphasizing the closed curve. Two chairs, with strong circular or ovoid forms and a Modernist feel, appear to be having a design conversation: *Gyro* by Matthew Harding and Greg Miller's *Hard Rocker* (both on p. 81). Another piece, *Compass*, by Vivian Beer (p. 82), perhaps working off a drafting stool, uses legs that resemble compasses. What better way to suggest architecture and curves than with this drafting tool?

Gently undulating curves characterize Jake Antonelli's *Daydreamer* chaise (p. 76). It has the beautiful simplicity of certain basket forms or lashed campcraft furniture. Another elegant, undulating form is *Chaise* by Jennifer Anderson (pgs. 72 and 77),

updating the much-explored lounge chair form with a thick pad of felt; it is a study in simplicity.

Another piece worked in felt is *Elephant Seating* by Ryuki Miyagi (p. 77). At first glance, you have the impression that the chair would be shipped as a flat piece of felt with folding instructions as in an origami book. The ultimate portable or small apartment chair, it is a more tailored version of Gaetano Pesce's experiments. What more symbolic set of curves exist than those that form a heart shape? Glenn P. Paculba uses a vivid, red, heart-shaped seat, poising it on a dark stand with a curving half-heart joining the two in *Sweetheart Chair* (p. 82). The words "bottomless love" spring to mind. In a historic context one might contrast this warm heart with a stool of similar design, the well-known, cold, tractor-seat stool (*Mezzadro*) designed by Achille Castiglioni and Pier Giacomo Castiglioni. The closest relative in the exhibition to the *Sweetheart Chair* would have to be Erik A. Wolken's *Torso #3* (p. 83), a cabinet with sleek, dark, curving lines.

Several works in the exhibition riff off early American furniture. A. K. Phillips's *1795 Rhode Island Braced Bowback Windsor Armchair* (p. 80) provides a time-tested design of perfectly proportioned, pleasing curves. The wow of it is to learn that it is a miniature (just under ten inches high), a technical and aesthetic achievement. Two related tables, Garrett Hack's *Side Table* and Richard H. Oedel's *Serpentine Card Table* (both on p. 80) also strike traditional and formal notes. They deal with the curve in the most restrained and elegant way, a slight bowing on their fronts.

A further departure from classic forms, techniques and materials is the energetic (and frankly awe-inspiring) *Card Table* by Alf Sharp (p. 81). This *tour de force* of marquetry and inlay embraces early American furniture while challenging its formality: note the updated leg treatment, the satisfying organic asymmetry of the table top, gorgeous wood grains, and visual images (Sharp also created a companion using Colorcore instead of wood veneers).

A version of traditional furniture design more related to 1950s biomorphism is found in Kevin

Irvin's segmented dresser *Red Orbitz* (p. 77). The title suggests an extraterrestrial form complete with splaying legs and antenna-like finial. A closer look reveals the fine craftsmanship displayed in the drawer fronts.

You will see throughout the exhibition that almost all of the furniture pieces bear titles, reminding us of the deep connection to the art and design world that they all bear. Whether built of contemporary or traditional forms, "Curv-iture" serves as a satisfying vehicle to convey the imaginative and eclectic thrust of studio furniture makers today. ♖

Palindrome Birthday Brocade Table
by Jill Henrietta Davis of Providence, RI
Glass, mirroring
22 inches x 24 inches x 24 inches, 2002
(detail at top)

Jill Davis does a lot of glass tables with a brocade pattern on the top, but the top for this one was slumped successfully on her 33rd birthday, hence the name, *Palindrome Birthday Brocade Table*. The brocade pattern is sandblasted into the glass and the legs are hand-blown. Both the top and the legs are silvered to give the table a lustrous effect. She likes the form of the occasional table as a means of expressing her personality. She has made about twenty-five tables in this series, most of them with a brocade pattern, but some are decorated with American flags or clock faces.

Benny Goodman
by Cosmo A. Barbaro of Lafayette, LA
Redwood burl, cherry, ebony, glass
25 inches x 17 inches x 17 inches, 2002

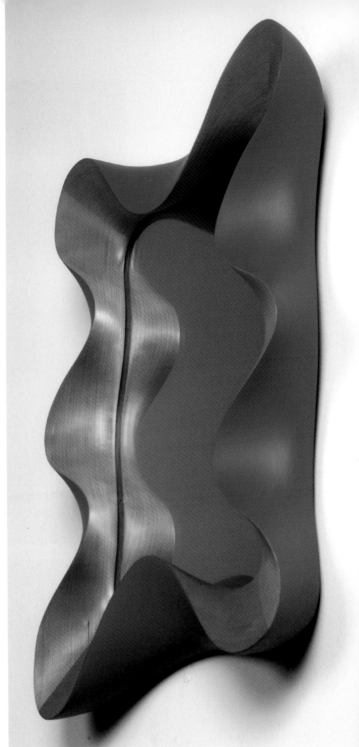

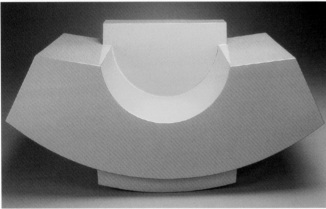

Steel Rocker by Isaac Arms of Madison, WI
Steel with powder coating and rust patina
28 inches x 60 inches x 31 inches, 2003

Isaac Arms describes his chair as a study of volume and form in a minimalist way. The idea of a rocking chair grew out of the evolution of the base from a rectangular pedestal to a curved form echoing the curves of the seat and base. Only when the chair gently rocks sideways is it possible to sense the hefty 200-pound weight of the chair thus giving added emphasis to its imposing mass. After carefully and laboriously grinding the welded edge joints, he applied gun bluing to accentuate the curves. Wanting to make the piece sing, he chose yellow as the most eye-popping color. Usually employed in industrial applications, powder coating is applied by spraying powdered pigment on the surface, which is held there by an electrical charge until baked on in a 400-degree oven. The chair obviously caught the eye of the "Curv-iture" judges, who gave it their Award of Excellence. Another piece by Arms appears on page 22.

Blue Taffy Mirror
by David Hurwitz of Randolph, VT
Cherry, paint, mirror
15 inches x 15 inches x 2 inches, 2002

The title of *Blue Taffy Mirror* certainly captures the bold plasticity of this piece. The idea grew out of other projects where Hurwitz used the twisted motif on table legs and lamp bases. He roughs out the shape with a band saw and carving gouges, and then sands and finishes the two-inch thick frame. Adding the paint was an accident. Trying to cover up a blemish in the cherry, he found that the blue paint added a pleasing contrast with the red of the wood.

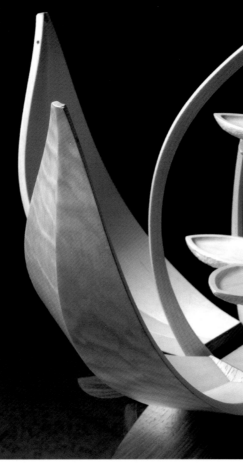

far left: Lotus Box
by Michael Craigdallie
of Nanaimo, BC, Canada
Quilted western maple,
paudauk, maple
43 inches x 18 inches x
18 inches, 2002
(open detail at left)

Michael Craigdallie's *Lotus Box* won
the People's Choice Award at the
23rd Annual Box and Container show
in Seattle, WA. The plant idea grew
naturally from his love of plants, and
the lotus form he picked up from
reading Eastern philosophy. The
leaves presented the trickiest
challenge, requiring fifty different
jigs to form the bent laminations.
The legs are cut from solid wood,
but the ribs between the leaves are
steam-bent. He chose paduak for the
base for its red color, which has now
faded to brown, and quilted maple
for the bud so that its wild grain
pattern covered the joint between
the veneers. The bud spins on a
dowel rising from the base, and the
leaves fold down to expose shelves.

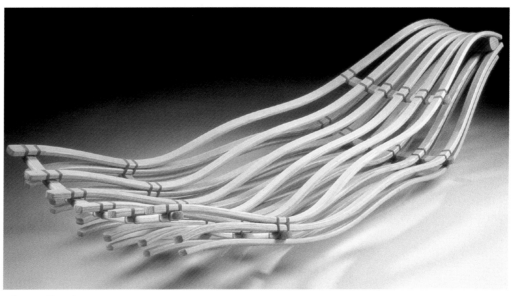

above: Daydreamer
by Jake Antonelli of Gatlinburg, TN
Ash, yellowheart, waxed twine
16 inches x 16 inches x 48 inches, 2002
(detail at left)

right, and on p. 72: Chaise
by Jennifer Anderson of San Diego, CA
Industrial felt, birch plywood,
maple veneer, steel cable
20 inches x 26 inches x 85 inches, 2004

Jennifer Anderson spent a semester
in Sweden at the school started by Carl
Malmsten, where she discovered *tovad
ull* (felted wool), a handmade version
of industrial felt found in this country.
Using about ten yards of the material,
she punched six hundred holes along the
edges and drew a cable through them
to achieve the pleated surface of her
chaise. By varying the distance between
the holes she was able to control the
thickness of the seat. She cut the four
ribs that form the frame out of Baltic birch
plywood and joined them with metal
rods. The nuts which secure the rods to
the outside ribs are covered by a second
piece of plywood glued over the first.

above: Elephant Seating
by Ryoki Miyagi of Princeton, NJ
Industrial felt
29 inches x 29 inches x 33 inches, 2003

left: Red Orbitz
by Kevin Irvin of Phoenix, AZ
Bubinga
50 inches x 16 inches x 14 inches,
2004

Bubinga has a reddish cast,
and the four oval drawers look
like orbits, hence the name,
Red Orbitz. Irvin got the idea for
this piece from walking around
Portland, Oregon, and noticing
café and hotel signs in oval
patterns. He combined this
concept with elements from
a 1950s style, two-tier coffee
table, particularly the tapered
legs, which were a signature
of mid-century Modern furniture.
Instead of typical 1950s metal
glides, he meticulously cuts his
out of wood. Rather than set up
the lathe, Irvin found it easier to
hand-shape the glides, and even
the tapered legs and the ball pulls
as well. Scallop-shaped veneers
were glued to the drawer fronts
to add texture.

left: *In the Realm of the Senses*
by Derek Secor Davis of Boulder, CO
Pigmented epoxy, cottonwood
branches, ash, fir, poplar, acrylic
35 inches x 19 inches x 48 inches, 2004
(detail below)

This table is about nature and how
life reproduces—sort of a poetic take
on sexuality. Two spheres or eggs
support two hemispheres that are
merging into each other, or dividing,
depending on how you look at them.
To reinforce the theme of nature and
reproduction, found twigs branch out
across the surface. Davis glued the
twigs to the tabletop and covered them
with epoxy, which he then sanded to
expose the twigs. He hollowed out the
egg forms to reduce the chance of
splitting and checking. The legs are
bent-laminated oak and ash. For both
economical and philosophical reasons,
Davis made the entire piece from
found and recycled wood.

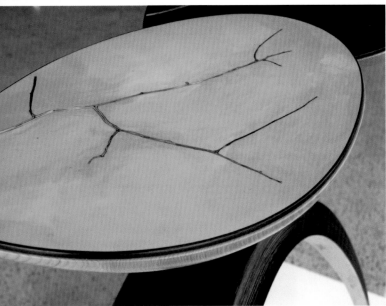

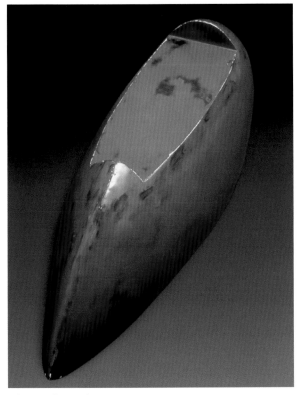

above: *Speedo*
by Marc D'Estout of Santa Cruz, CA
Painted aluminum
16.5 inches x 59.5 inches x 18 inches, 2003

above: Vera by Kim Kelzer
of Freeland, WA
Birch plywood, mahogany, milk paint
36 inches x 18 inches x 25 inches, 2002
(detail at right)

Kim Kelzer said that *Vera* just looked like
the right name for this telephone table.
One of a series of three, the others have
chalkboard tops for writing messages.
The legs attach to the sides of the drawer
section in a manner reminiscent of
Jacques Ruhlmann's furniture from the
1920s. The scalloped ruffles at the top
of the legs are cut from a turned bowl
and painted. The ruffle theme repeats
at the top of the legs and on the drawer
pulls. The legs are decorated to suggest
clothes and the feet offset-turned to
emphasize the accessorizing theme.

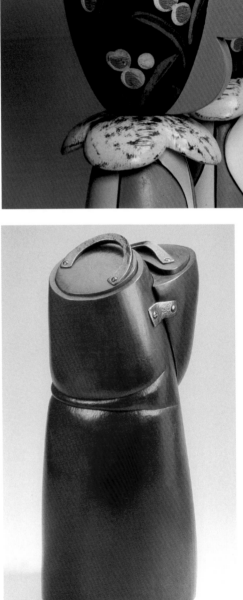

right: Bear
by Ashley Jameson Eriksmoen
of Oakland, CA
Mahogany, milk paint, acrylic
28 inches x 15 inches x 14 inches, 2002

above: Boat Table
by Chris Bowman
of Bedford, IN
Mahogany, poplar, milk paint
25 inches x 20 inches
x 8 inches, 2004

Side Table
by Garrett Hack of Thetford Center, VT
Maple, cherry, ebony, holly
29.5 inches x 40 inches x 15 inches, 2004

1795 Rhode Island Braced
Bowback Windsor Armchair
by A. K. Phillips of Shawneetown, IL
Osage orange, milk paint
9.875 inches x 4.75 inches x 5.5 inches, 2002

Stealth Chair
by Heath Matysek-Snyder of Madison, WI
Maple, plywood, steel
40 inches x 21 inches x 25 inches, 2002

Serpentine Card Table
by Richard H. Oedel of Salem, MA
Mahogany, crotch birch, makore,
holly, Gabon ebony
29 inches x 36 inches x 18 inches, 2003

below, and left:
Gyro by Matthew Harding
of Canberra, Australia
Stainless steel, upholstery
43 inches x 43 inches x 30 inches, 2002

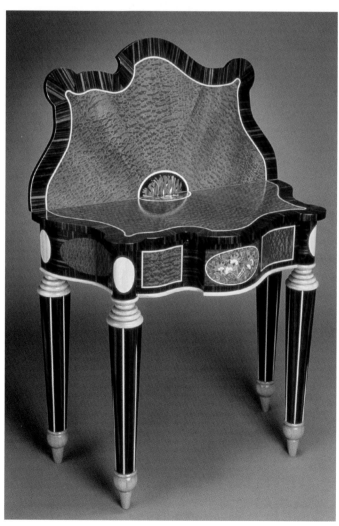

Hard Rocker
by Greg Miller of Ephrata, PA
Corian
38 inches x 24 inches x 40 inches, 2003

Greg Miller is a certified Dupont Corian fabricator installing kitchen counter tops and shower stalls. He saw an elliptical rocker in steel on television one day and decided to replicate it in Corian. The seat and back is a single sheet of Corian plastic thermoformed in a 350-degree oven. The rockers and the joints where the seat and the rockers come together are formed by sixty-six different pieces of plastic which are glued up, very much like the stack-lamination techniques using wood, and then laboriously shaped and sanded to the smooth curves of the final product.

Card Table
by Alf Sharp of Woodbury, TN
Macassar ebony, sapele, sycamore
30 inches x 33 inches x 17 inches, 2003

above, right: Compass by Vivian Beer
of Bloomfield Hills, MI
Forged steel, mahogany
26 inches x 30 inches x 26 inches, 2003
(detail above)

For this chair Vivian Beer combined the concept of an old
office swivel chair with eighteenth-century forged tools
she had seen at Colonial Williamsburg. In effect, she
made the chair out of tools employed in the design
of the chair itself. Thus, two giant dividers, used to lay
out curves, form the legs. The height, and even the angle
of the seat, can be adjusted by spreading the dividers.
A major challenge in the fabrication process was aligning
the holes in the dividers for the curved seat rails. She
pierced the dividers with a driftpin, or punch, spreading
the metal to provide added thickness for strength. The
mahogany seat and back, which mediate between the
sitter and the hard steel, were fabricated with equal care.
Shaped on a lathe, these elements are subtly concave
on the back and undersides and convex on the fronts.

right: Sweetheart Chair
by Glenn P. Paculba
of San Diego, CA
Steel, silk
33 inches x 17 inches x 43 inches,
2003

left, and below: Torso #3
by Erik A. Wolken
of Chapel Hill, NC
Mahogany, cherry,
digital imagery, milk paint
33 inches x 20 inches
x 1 inch, 2004

Part of a series of four *Torso* cabinets, this piece combines a three-dimensional form with two-dimensional digital images inside, a vague reference to public and private space. Serving as a sort of reliquary cabinet for sacred objects, the inside contains four images that document a family trip Wolken took on the SS *Rotterdam* when he was a child. The four photographs are pixelated from faint to clear to recall fading memories. The mahogany cabinet is painted multiple times with red and black, and rubbed between coats to expose the striations of the wood.

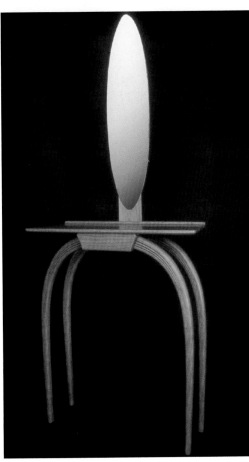

Mirror Hall Table
by David Zawistowski of Ruby, NT
Cherry, black walnut
72 inches x 30 inches x 12 inches, 2003
(detail above)

David Zawistowski's *Mirror Hall Table* has a clear anthropological quality, but initially he was mainly interested in the interplay of curves. The legs are bent laminations with inset spears of black walnut to emphasize their shape. He thought about curving the shelf as well but wanted the piece to be functional. He also considered a drawer, but the space was taken up by the leg joints and the mirror connection. To avoid a huge chunk of wood on the back, the mirror is supported with a board coved on the edge and tapering to the thickness of the mirror itself.

This bench was a class project at Sheridan College in Ontario, Canada, to build a piece of furniture to fit any space. Finley was fascinated with rocking chairs, and this led her to the concept of a rocking bench. The strips are laminated, but she matched the oak grain so well that they look steam-bent. She split the rails to reduce the mass and added wedges at the ends for strength. Each of the rails is the same length so when they are joined to the curved rockers they form a gentle depression at the top of the arc, which repeats the curve of the rockers.

below: The Rocking Bench
by Lara Finley
of Mississauga, ON, Canada
White oak
18 inches x 25 inches x 6 inches, 2003

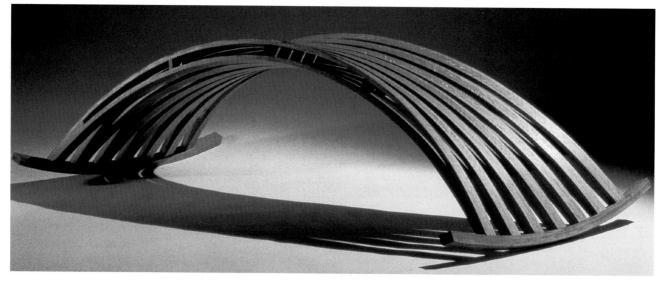

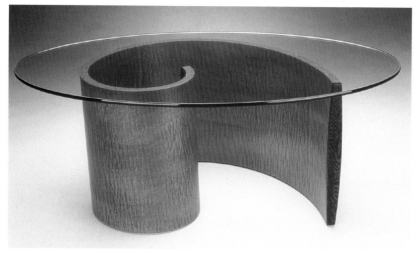

above: Spiral Table
by Richard Judd of Belleville, WI
Pommele, sapele veneer,
bending ply, wenge, glass
18 inches x 30 inches x 50 inches,
2003

right: A Simple Chair Prototype
by Mark Koons of Wheatland, WY
Curly cherry veneer, kangaroo hide
31 inches x 26 inches x 22 inches,
2003

A Simple Chair is really not so simple. Mark Koons worked out the design over five years, first experimenting with steam-bending but in the end using bent-lamination and veneers. It contains 218 pieces and requires 50 clamps to shape the parts around forms. The seat, which is wider than normal in the tradition of thrones, also allows the user to squirm a little during long meetings. The seat is covered in kangaroo hide which is flexible, thin, and holds its shape well. Leather pads glued to the bottom of the feet protect the floor when the chair is moved around.

Tendril
by Jefferson Shallenberger of Fort Bragg, CA
Mahogany, jarrah, redwood burl, holly, silver
29 inches x 49 inches x 25 inches, 2003
(details below)

A friend named the companion chair *Tendril* as a joke, but the bent laminated legs suggest just that. This desk started out as a standup model with straight legs, but when Shallenberger started to reconfigure it as a sit down desk he felt the straight legs were too boring. He used book-matched light mahogany veneer for the writing surface, and the grain continues down over the drawer fronts. A band of Australian jarrah wood with holly inlay accentuates the curved top, which is also echoed in the curved base. He cut and shaped the silver pulls himself. The careful workmanship and striking design won an Award of Excellence. For more of Shallenberger's work, see page 31.

Reinterpreting the Windsor Chair

Traditional chair-making techniques prove
surprisingly well-suited to body-conscious design

by Galen Cranz

On the basis of my having written an interdisciplinary book about chair design, I was invited to visit the Penland School of Crafts in the fall of 2002 where I was introduced to Curtis Buchanan, a chair-maker from Tennessee. After hearing his eloquent account of bringing a sustainable craft practice from Appalachia to Latin America, I was inspired to ask him if he would consider teaching a course with me at Penland about chair-making from a body-conscious point of view. In June 2004 we offered such a class, described as exploring the consequences

of body-conscious design for traditional chair-making. This essay reports on this experience.

Body-conscious Design

The term body-conscious means the body and mind are related parts of a single system. By including the mind in our thinking about the body, we go beyond mere ergonomics (that is, the measuring of body parts) so that we can include educational and philosophical ideas about the body. Applied to design, body-consciousness means including

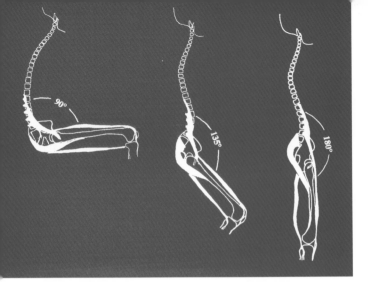

above: Right-angle seating produces a C-shaped spine. Perching is halfway between sitting and standing, but retains the postural advantage of standing—the S-shaped spine.

left: Peter Galbert made this Windsor-style perching stool following the design he developed along with the other two Penland instructors, Curtis Buchanan and Galen Cranz. It's shown against an ancestor, a classic American Windsor chair made by Michael Dunbar in 1985. Photo by John Kelsey.

ergonomic, psychological, and cultural perspectives all together. Body-conscious design is broader than ergonomics because it is not only focused on the biomechanics of the body, but also on the psychological and cultural feelings and beliefs that a person brings to understanding the body in relationship to the environment. This integrated perspective has been called the somatic perspective, which I came to through the Alexander Technique. It is what informed my thinking in my book *The Chair: Rethinking Culture, Body and Design* (New York: W. W. Norton & Co., 1998). Another movement educator, Paul Linden, defines "somatic" as involving "the whole human being, focusing in a practical way on the interactions of posture, movement, emotion, self-concept, and cultural values." (Paul Linden, "Somatic Literacy: Bringing Somatic Education into Physical Education," JOPERD September 1994, page 16.)

Galen Cranz, Ph.D., teaches body-conscious design in the Department of Architecture, University of California, Berkeley, and is the author of The Chair: Rethinking Culture, Body and Design *(New York: W. W. Norton & Co., 1998). Dr. Cranz presented a version of this paper at The Furniture Society's 2004 conference in Savannah, GA.*

Implications for Chair Design

Chair designers may be surprised or dismayed or even relieved to hear me say that the chair itself is the problem, not good chair design or bad chair design. The right-angle seated posture creates problems for our lower backs that cannot be designed away. The pelvis tends to roll backward, flattening the lumbar curve and creating problems for lumbar disks and distorting the spine all the way up to the head and neck. The sit-stand position halfway between sitting and standing, which I have called the "perch" position, is fundamentally better than the right-angle seated posture. That said, it is also true that some conventional chairs are better than others. Body-conscious requirements for chairs include the following:

- both feet should be flat on the floor;
- the legs should not be crossed;
- knees should be lower than hip sockets;
- pelvis should not be rolled backward;
- the spine should retain natural curves, appearing straight upright overall;
- the chest should be open rather than collapsed;
- the head should be balanced on top of the spine, not resting back and down on it;
- I should be able to look at work or at people within a fifteen degree cone from the eyebrows down, and I should not be forced to look too far up or down.

What does this unusual point of view mean for traditional chairs? Is body-conscious design too radical for a vernacular tradition in chair design like the Windsor?

The Windsor

For a two-week workshop at Penland a master teacher has an assistant. Curtis Buchanan chose chair-maker Pete Galbert, with whom he had worked previously. The two of them decided to use the Windsor as the starting point for all student projects because they wanted to narrow the range of techniques, in anticipation of putting their

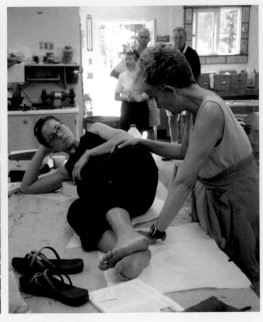

far left, top: Here is the log from which the students split all their posts and rungs for the exercise in somatic chair making.

far left, bottom: Students used shave-horses and draw-knives to shape the riven legs and posts of their chairs. These techniques produce strong parts with no wood grain run-out.

left: Galen Cranz explains a biomechanical principle to Amelia Brooks. Cranz took measurements of each student's body in order to develop dimensions for the class exercise in somatic chair-making. Photo by Peter Galbert.

attention on the new and unpredictable influences of my theories about comfortable seating. The essential characteristic of the Windsor is that the seat is the anchor for both the legs and back, but the legs and the back nevertheless are structurally independent of one another.

Buchanan teaches green woodworking by starting with a log, which he selects from a local lumber mill and drives to the Penland campus where students help saw it into lengths and then hand-split it into billets. Students worked on shave-horses to create the legs and arms for their chairs. The seats were carved. Some students learned how to bend wood by steaming it for their chair backs or for unconventional supports. All the joints were fastened without glue, screws, or nails, using the traditional technique of inserting a dried tenon into a relatively moist mortise.

My contributions were to describe these new theoretical principles of body-conscious design, and to set up exercises for experiential learning. *The Chair* had been assigned in advance and I supplemented it with two slide lectures. I helped each student and the other instructors develop physical, experiential awareness of how these principles are at work in their own bodies. Finally, I measured each person bio-mechanically to help

them make decisions about the sizes of their chair elements: leg length, seat depth, back length and angle.

Woodworking classes are limited to nine students, and due to a last-minute cancellation we worked with eight students, four men and four women; some of their work is shown in the snapshots. Four of the designs would be recognizable as traditional Windsor chairs. However, even these are unconventional in several different ways, as a result of new principles that we applied to this vernacular form.

An important principle is that there is a world of difference between enlarging the angle between the seat and the back by sending the back backward, versus enlarging it by canting the seat forward. Conventionally, designers slant the chair back backward between five and ten degrees, but this has the consequence of creating a C-shaped slump in the spine. When the spine follows the trajectory of the chair back in space, the head has to come forward, thereby distorting the relationship between neck, head, and spine into a C-shape. Our students kept the back spindles at close to a right angle to the seat, and tipped the seat forward—at an angle that I determined for each student individually by using a mock-up seat on a shave-horse.

For people taller than 5 foot 6 inches, the forward cant of the seat usually meant that it had to be higher than the conventional seventeen to eighteen inches. For the tallest man in our class, the legs were twenty-one inches and they should have been even taller in order to get his knees significantly lower than his hip sockets, a convenient rule of thumb for maintaining the lumbar curve. Such a chair for him would be stool height for most people. However, he wanted this dining room chair not to be his exclusively, but rather something his petite wife could use occasionally. He could have proceeded to design a smaller chair for her, but perhaps he did not like the vision of different sized chairs around the table, either for reasons of convention or for more personal reasons of not wanting to call attention to his height. His situation underscores the importance of the somatic perspective because it takes into account people's beliefs and feelings as well as their ergonomic measurements.

Two other students also designed stationary Windsor chairs with appropriate modifications for their size and the principles I have described. One other did the same but as a rocker. In addition, she decided to make a radically short seat, partly because she herself is short, but primarily because weight should be transferred from the body to the seat through the sit bones, not through flesh, and therefore, the seat need be only deep enough to comfortably catch the sit bones.

In all of these chairs the back spindles were set into the seat to be more upright than usual. Moreover, they were set far enough away from the pelvis to make room for the bulge of the buttocks. Alternatively, the back spindles could be steam-bent to make buttocks room. The purpose of doing this is to have back support where it is wanted— along the spine. If the spindles are too close to the buttocks, the spine reaches backward to find support, thereby flattening the lumbar curve, which in turn pushed the pelvis, neck, and head forward.

The remainder of the student designs departed from the conventional chair paradigm, producing

Joe McArdle created this taller-than-average dining table chair. Ideally his knees would be lower than his hips (in order to recreate the lumbar curve), but raising the seat would make it too high for his petite wife— a social constraint on body-conscious design.

Shannon Oesch created an unusually shallow seat, which frees the thighs from pressure, especially appreciated by short people, that is, most women.

Brian McGee exploited steam-bending to create this perch. Because the sitter can sit at various points, the perch can accommodate taller and shorter people.

Heather Miller achieved the forward tilt by shaping the seat, and by the angle of attachment to its single curved pedestal.

Hannah Whitaker's stool creates a forward tilt by the way the seat is set, the way it is shaped, and the differential leg length. The finish is black milk paint.

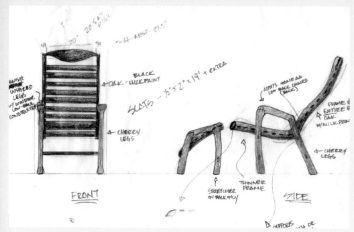

Working sketch for a two-part lounge chair
by Amelia Brooks.

instead perches, a lounge chair and stools such
as the ones shown on the previous page. Three
of these took advantage of the capacity of green
woodworking technology to create pronounced
curves. Brian McGee created two parallel curves
joined by a ladder of perching "shelves." When
the sit-stand position (knees at an oblique relation
to the spine) is rotated in space, it produces a
configuration that we would recognize as a lounge
chair. One student decided to explore this option
using large pieces of bent wood. Another used
the steam box to create a single curved support
for a shaped seat set at an angle appropriate for
perching. This scheme required an unconventional
flared foot, to ground and stabilize the pedestal, so
she carved it as well as the seat. In some senses no
more than a stool, this design looks somewhat like
a tractor seat. It was still a "Windsor" in that the
chair seat remained independent of its support.

Two stools were taller than conventional chairs,
closer to the height of stools used at kitchen
counters and bars. In addition to being tall to
support the perch position, the seats were canted
forward. One of these stools was produced by a
student who painted it with black milk paint, and
the other was produced as a collaboration between
the three instructors, left a natural wood, and
sold at the school auction.

In all cases the seats were carved to enhance a
forward slope, but they also were carved shallowly
from side to side so as to not inhibit movement.
Traditional Windsor seats might be carved to hold
the pelvis in place, but this is antithetical to another
principle of body-conscious design, namely, that
movement is more important than supporting
any single position. Windsor green woodworking
technology has the additional advantage of
producing unpadded seating, so the weight
transfers through bones. Padding presses the
flesh around the sit bones so that flesh takes
on a load-bearing function for which it is not
designed, reducing circulation.

Summary and Conclusions

A summary of the somatic principles needed to
modify the Windsor according to our experience
might be useful.

Conventional chairs are too tall for most women
and children and about half of the male population,
so a conventional right-angle seated Windsor chair
could be lower than seventeen or eighteen inches.
However, the right-angle seated posture is
detrimental to the lumbar spine. Therefore, the
Windsor should approach a perch height with the
pelvis rotated forward and the knees lower than the
hip sockets. The conventional seventeen to eighteen
inch height would work as a perch for the men,
women, and children who currently suffer in
conventional chairs. For others who are taller than
average, greater height is needed, but only if
accompanied by the forward slant of the seat and
an upright, not backward-sloped, chair back. If the
chair is high enough and the seat shaped and tilted
correctly, the lumbar curve is automatically in place
and it is easy to sit upright without any back support
whatsoever. This argues for chairs without a back—
in other words, perching stools.

At Penland we learned that traditional chair types
can be modified to be more responsive to the body
while remaining recognizable as part of a tradition
in craft process as well as a visual look. Being
recognizable is important so that people don't
need to be told how to use the seating apparatus.
If they recognize it as a seat, whether stool, chair,
or lounge, they will not feel disoriented and will
feel competent. If the seat is too unusual to be
recognized, most people will avoid using it and
any physiological benefits will be lost.

Chair Recommendations

Specifications

- For conventional right-angled sitting, seat height no greater than the top of your knee minus two inches.

- Forward-tilt the seat (the more the task takes you forward, the more the seat should tilt forward); you will also require a forward slope for the work surface, and a computer at eye level; the logic of forward-tilt seats argues for raising seat height significantly (four to six inches), which creates a perching chair rather than a conventional chair.

- Firm textured surface, upholstered but not more than one-half inch to one inch depth.

- Flat, uncontoured seat.

- Butt space between seat and backrest.

- Midback support or full back, neck, and head support excepting butt space.

- Flat, planar backrest.

- Armrests for support if reading, typing, keyboarding, painting, or other similar activities.

Use

- Both feet should be flat on floor (helps organize spine upward).

- Legs not crossed (helps protect pelvis).

- Knees should be lower than hip sockets (takes strain off lower back).

- Pelvis should not be rolled back.

- Spine should retain natural curves, but appear straight overall.

- Chest should be open rather than collapsed.

- Head should be balanced on top of spine, not resting back and down on it.

- Eyes should be able to look at work or people within a fifteen degree cone, not forced to look too far up or down.

What can everyone do?

- Practice autonomous sitting and perching, without chairbacks. One of the easiest ways to wean oneself from chairs is to start using stools more often.

- Use a variety of postures, including lying down, standing, squatting, and crawling.

- Rather than let the spine sag in a slump when tired, decide to rest it by lying down in the constructive rest position. Lie down on a firm surface so that the spine can extend itself and the rib cage can open out against this resistant plane. The surface should be firm enough to keep the body from sinking down, which means firmer than most beds. Avoid any surface that curves. At the same time, bring the knees up. Bend the elbows and bring both hands over the midriff in order to let the shoulders slide back and the joints open at the shoulder, elbows and wrists.

- For tasks that require bending over, use the position of mechanical advantage. The waist is not a hinge. When a person needs to bend over, he or she should instead flex the knees, ankles, and hip joints.

- Use reading and writing stands. The height of the work surface should be derived from the height of the seat surface.

Reprinted with permission from *The Chair: Rethinking Culture, Body, and Design* by Galen Cranz (New York: W.W. Norton & Co., 1998).

Furniture-maker Peter Handler of Philadelphia applied Galen Cranz's ideas in the design and construction of this upholstered perching stool, made of anodized aluminum.

Furniture-maker Michael Podmaniczy of Winterthur, DE, attempted to integrate somatic design principles with the eighteenth-century bent-laminated chair-making techniques devised by Samuel Gragg of Boston.

Furniture-maker Michael Puryear of New York City has experimented with this adjustable-height wobble stool, which incorporates some of the principles of somatic chair design.

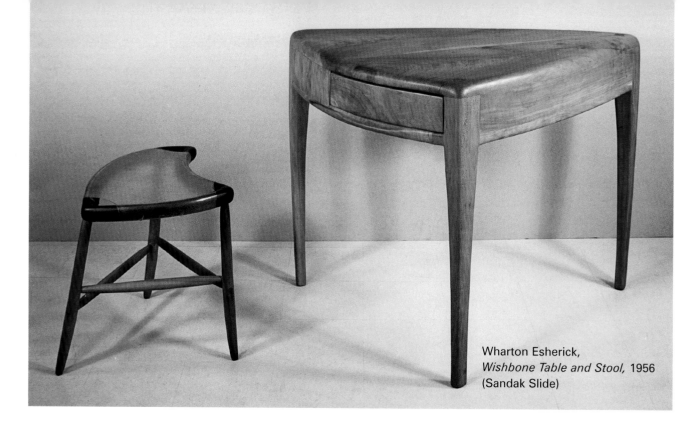

Wharton Esherick,
Wishbone Table and Stool, 1956
(Sandak Slide)

Who Makes Studio Furniture?

Interviews with 109 well-known artists

by Oscar P. Fitzgerald

Although the roots of the American[1] craft movement date to the late nineteenth century, the contemporary reincarnation of studio furniture can be traced to the 1920s and the career of Wharton Esherick, the patriarch of studio furniture makers. A serious look at the field as a whole is long overdue. With most of the key players still alive, now is the time to interview these makers and answer questions about their careers, how they were trained, how they designed and produced their furniture, and how they marketed it. By compiling this information it will be possible to take a snapshot of the field and record how it has prospered over the past fifty years.

Methodology

At first glance, the task appears daunting. Over time the Furniture Society has enrolled almost 2,000 members who identify themselves as makers. The total number of professional furniture makers nationwide could exceed twenty thousand.[2]

In order to identify a manageable group to interview, the first step was to identify the hundred or so most influential craftsmen and women who have shaped the field as teachers, innovators, and trendsetters.

One objective measure of relative influence is to the count number of times a maker's name appears in a variety of publications in the craft field such as *American Craft, Woodwork*, and *Fine Woodworking* as well as in the major books and catalogs of studio furniture exhibits published since 1950.[3] Although written material was given primary importance in the selection process, other criteria such as teaching positions held, work in museum collections, and peer recognition through awards and honors was considered as well.

While this is not a perfectly objective approach, it is a widely accepted evaluation technique and has more validity than the purely subjective judgments all too often used to select participants in juried

left to right: William and Mary High Chair, Miguel Gomez-Ibanez, 2000. *Wall Flower,* Christine Enos, 2000. *Mermaids' Shadows,* Tommy Simpson, 1995 (*Two Looks to Home*). *Louise,* Bob Trotman, 1997 (Renwick Gallery of the Smithsonian American Art Museum). *Writing Desk,* Peter Dean, 1983.

shows or exhibits. This methodology is, however, biased towards those makers who have made a conscious and successful effort to publicize their work. Some makers, such as Thomas Lacagnina, a teacher at Alfred University, are important but are not well-known outside the field. The methodology also is naturally biased toward makers in wood, since *Fine Woodworking* and other such publications obviously focus on that medium. Although the inclusion of *Woodwork* helps to identify West Coast makers, the study may not have given makers from this area adequate representation.

The preliminary list of the 109 most influential makers was developed by Charlene Johnson as an independent study project in my History of Studio Furniture class offered in the Smithsonian/Parsons Masters Program in the Decorative Arts. Her study and subsequent research identified 388 makers with one or more mentions in 79 books and 87 articles.[4]

Dr. Oscar Fitzgerald earned his M.A. and Ph.D. in history from Georgetown University and served as director of the Navy Museum in Washington, DC, until he decided to pursue full-time his passion as a furniture historian and decorative arts consultant. He is currently on the faculty of the Smithsonian Institution/Parsons School master's program in the decorative arts, where he developed and teaches a core course on the studio furniture movement. His book, Four Centuries of American Furniture *(Iola, WI: Krause Publications, 1995), which includes coverage of the studio furniture movement, is a standard reference work in the field. In 2004 he was awarded a prestigious James Renwick Research Fellowship, which funded the research for this essay.*

Of these, 155 makers were covered in two or more publications. Not surprisingly, Wendell Castle had the most mentions with 31. Extra weight was given to makers whose furniture is displayed in major museum collections such as the Renwick Gallery of the Smithsonian American Art Museum, the Museum of Fine Arts Boston, the Mint Museum in Charlotte, North Carolina, and to those who were the recipients of National Endowment for the Arts grants. Several gallery owners, collectors, and other specialists in the field, who graciously agreed to review the list, provided a final screen.[5]

Three categories of craftsmen were excluded from this study: those who produce fine reproductions of historical furniture, those who are involved with industrial design for limited production, and those artists who occasionally make furniture without it being their primary medium. None of these categories is finely defined, and they overlap. For example, Miguel Gomez-Ibanez makes carefully crafted reproductions, but a closer look at his work shows that it is really more than that. He often is making subtle statements similar to the best of narrative furniture. An analysis of his William and Mary style high chair reveals that it is a bit over scale—just the impression a child would have when looking up at the seat from the floor.

In the industrial design category, Gregg Fleishman's *Zigzag Chair* was initially marketed through galleries specializing in craft, and he has developed multiple versions of his unique chair. While he originally made the prototypes individually in his own studio,

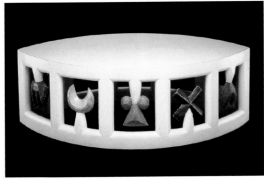

left to right: Okavango Bench, Colin Reid, 1995. *Dining Table,* Rory McCarthy, 1976 (Renwick Gallery of the Smithsonian American Art Museum). *Ten,* Randy Shull, 1997 (Renwick Gallery of the Smithsonian American Art Museum).

turning out up to one hundred copies a year, his primary goal is to produce these chairs in even larger numbers on an assembly line. The same is true of Peter Danko's innovative, one-piece plywood chairs, which are now produced by a major furniture manufacturer. Some studio furniture makers do engage in limited production work, but it does not represent the majority of their output as it does in the case of Peter Danko, Gregg Fleishman, and others in this category.

The category of artist is more problematic because most studio furniture-makers consider themselves artists. Many artists have discovered the immediacy of furniture and use it as a means to connect with the viewer. Their intent is not to make a functional object but to convey an idea. The distinction blurs, however, when looking, for example, at the *Rock Chair* of Scott Burton. It is a piece of sculpture, but it is also fully meant to sit on. On the other hand, the work of Tommy Simpson is about telling a story but, even if minimally, his pieces do function as furniture. In the end, it is the intent of the maker that is the deciding factor. Is he or she making furniture that is artistic, or is the furniture being used purely as a medium for the message?

After refining the list, the next step was to develop a standardized questionnaire to gather information in telephone interviews about these craftsmen. The questionnaire was designed to elicit basic biographical data, shop practices, marketing strategies, aesthetic influences, design approaches, and trends in the field.[6] Of the names on the list,

five had died and thirteen had stopped making furniture altogether. Even in the case of the latter, however, all agreed to be interviewed. With regard to the former, they were of such stature that the written record was sufficiently detailed to complete the questionnaires without a personal interview.[7] Published sources and makers' resumes supplemented the information from the oral interviews. Although some of the interviews lasted up to two hours, 100 percent of the artists responded, and I am grateful for the time they spent to participate in this project. What follows are the results of the tabulation of the data from these 106 personal interviews.[8]

Biographical Data: Training and Employment

Three of the thirteen people who have stopped making furniture—Art Carpenter and Joyce and Edgar Anderson—are now in their eighties and have retired. Peter Dean stopped working in his shop because of health problems, although he is still designing furniture. Bob Trotman gave up furniture to become a full-time sculptor. Randy Shull has shifted his creative efforts to remaking the entire interior environment, after finding that people had a hard time placing his furniture in a conventionally decorated home. Kathran Siegel is teaching full-time while Rory McCarthy, Joanne Shima, Richard Ford, Fabiane Garcia, Yoko Shimitzu, and Collin Reid have left the furniture field altogether.

top row, left to right: Conoid Bench, George Nakashima, 1957 (Renwick Gallery of the Smithsonian American Art Museum). *Rocking Chair,* Sam Maloof, 1999 (Renwick Gallery of the Smithsonian American Art Museum). *Winged Bench,* Chris Martin, 2001.

bottom row, left to right: Upholstered Armchair, Robert Harman. *Hallway Table,* Steve Perrin, 1991 (Meridith Gallery). *Summer 99 Shell Desk,* Jere Osgood, 1999 (Museum of Fine Arts Boston). *Hidden Torso Chair,* Kathran Siegel.

So who are the people still working? They range in age from Christine Enos at age 34 to Sam Maloof at 88. Seventeen percent are women. Only five are under 40; 71 are between the ages of 40 and 60; and 23 are over 60, including Sam Maloof and James Krenov, who are still active even in their eighties. It is not surprising that few makers in their twenties and thirties show up in the survey since it is skewed toward established makers. With the exception of Randy Shull, who began selling furniture professionally at age 15, about two-thirds of the makers started their careers in their late twenties, but four makers made career changes in their forties: Steve Perrin, Robert Harman, Clifton Montieth, and James Krenov.

They live mostly in Massachusetts (19), California (18), New York (12), Pennsylvania (9), or Rhode Island (7), but the remaining 38 percent are scattered across the country in eleven different states. One explanation for the concentration in just five states is the presence of the major schools for American craftsmen: in New York the Rochester Institute of Technology (RIT); in California the programs at San Diego State University and the California College of Arts and Crafts in Oakland; the Pennsylvania College of Arts; and the Rhode Island School of Design (RISD). Many of the graduates from these programs have returned as teachers, or never left the area after graduation.

Only 28 percent of the makers were self-taught; half earned Bachelors or Masters degrees in Fine Arts, and the rest were trained in certificate programs such as the Program in Artisanry at Boston College or the Wendell Castle School. Twenty-two students received their degrees from either RIT or RISD while 16 others earned degrees from programs at San Diego State, the California College of Arts and Crafts, and the Philadelphia College of Art.[9] Before enrolling in these programs almost 80 percent of the makers had previous jobs or some exposure to the craft field, either as children or young adults.

top row, left to right: Three-Legged Stool, Tage Frid, 1982-83 (Renwick Gallery of the Smithsonian American Art Museum). *Side Chair,* Kristina Madsen, 1993 (Renwick Gallery of the Smithsonian American Art Museum). *Monkey Settee,* Judy Kinsley McKie, 1995 (Renwick Gallery of the Smithsonian American Art Museum). *Writers Cabinet,* Dale Broholm, 2002.

bottom row, left to right: Hepplewhite Dining Chair, Lee Schuette, 2002. *Adam and Eve Sharing an Hors d'Oeuvre Preceding Their New Career in Agribusiness,* Clifton Montieth, 1997. *Boetia Chair,* Paul Freundt, 1992. *One Voice,* Jon Brooks, 1998.

It is no secret how difficult it is to earn a living as a full-time furniture maker. Even among the most successful furniture craftsmen only about 40 percent work in the shop full-time. The rest augment their income with such occupations as antique restoration, product design, interior remodeling, contracting, landscape design, and especially teaching. In fact, 19 are full-time teachers and 29 teach part-time. Even among the 56 makers who do not teach, fully a quarter engage in some other part-time work.

Only about half the makers fit the stereotype of the lone cabinetmaker toiling in a small shop, and even these solitary workers on occasion rely on wives or shop-mates to lend a hand for heavy lifting. Eighteen have full-time assistants and others at times hire temporary help in order to complete a major commission or meet a gallery deadline. Thirty makers keep from two to four full-time shop

assistants and three—Wendell Castle, George Nakashima, and Albert Paley—have employed up to twelve helpers.

Shop Practices

Virtually all the craftsmen begin the design process with sketches. Two-thirds use drawings and models, but 17 go directly from models to production. A surprising number, 22—notably Garry Knox Bennett, Jon Brooks, and Daniel Mack—go directly from the sketchbook to the workbench without making shop drawings at all. Even among the makers who complete careful shop drawings, about half admit that their work routinely evolves from the original plans as they build the piece. By maintaining some flexibility to modify the plans, they hope to give the work a sense of freedom and spontaneity. The more experienced the maker, the less detailed drawings they need and the better their work. For this group, drawings and models are

left to right: Cylinder Fall Desk, Jere Osgood, 1989 (Renwick Gallery of the Smithsonian American Art Museum). *Radish Salad Bowl,* Craig Nutt, 1998 (Renwick Gallery of the Smithsonian American Art Museum). *Chair,* J. M. Syron and Bonnie Bishoff. *Eel Gig Chair,* Daniel Mack, 1992 (Renwick Gallery of the Smithsonian American Art Museum). *Musical Chair,* Eck Follen.

more often necessary for the client to understand the project than for the maker to have plans to follow.

At least 17 makers are using computer-aided design, but an equal number do not use such technology. Computer-generated plans are necessary for those few makers using computer-controlled laser-cutting technology, a technique that is growing in popularity. It is particularly useful for cutting metal and routing wood. Dale Broholm, for example, used it to cut out the letters he inlaid into the front of his *Writer's Cabinet.*

Output varies considerably depending on gallery commitments and commissions. But on average half the makers produce about one large piece a month. A quarter of the makers, however, pump out twice that number, and a few, like Sam Maloof and George Nakashima in their heydays, were producing over one hundred pieces of furniture a year. Almost half the makers confirm that they contract out at least some parts of their work. The most common operations are finishing and metal work that require special facilities and a large space, luxuries that most small shops do not have. Some makers subcontract limited amounts of casework, carving, drawer construction, veneer work, or turning. If they receive a large commission for chairs, for example, the craftsman might contract out the shaping of legs—repetitive tasks that do not require design decisions.

While about half the makers produce the whole range of furniture forms, 30 favor chairs, 16 prefer chests and 7 like to make tables. Jere Osgood and Wayne Marcoux specialize in desks. Two-thirds of the furniture makers craft only one-of-a-kind pieces, while the rest turn out limited editions of at least some of their work. The majority of the one-of-a-kind work is limited to fewer than ten copies, but at least nine makers have fabricated over 100 copies of some pieces over the course of their careers. Judy McKie has started making multiples of her furniture in bronze in order to save her body from the backbreaking labor of producing the same pieces over and over in wood.

Marketing Strategies

Making the furniture is one thing, selling it is a different challenge. About twice as much work is done on commission as on speculation. Some 14 percent do nothing but commissions while only 6 percent made work exclusively on speculation. Overall, 56 percent worked mostly on commission while 33 percent worked mostly on speculation. About 11 percent said that they divide their time evenly between commission and speculation.

Even though 90 percent of the respondents confirmed that they showed in galleries at some time in their careers, the trend seems to be toward more commissions for individuals and less speculative work for galleries. In the short run, this strategy increases the income of the maker

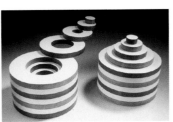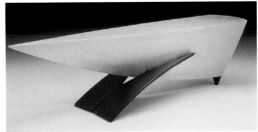

left to right: Botanical Reading Couch, Rosanne Somerson, 1992 (Renwick Gallery of the Smithsonian American Art Museum). *Wound Up,* Emi Ozawa, 2001. *Child's Chair,* Joanne Schima, 1987 (Renwick Gallery of the Smithsonian American Art Museum). *Long Coffee Table,* Charles Swanson, 1992.

who avoids gallery commissions of up to 50 percent, but in the long term, as galleries disappear, artists are not promoted and demand disappears. Just recently the John Elder Gallery in New York closed down. Only about a half-dozen galleries, which focus on furniture at the highest price point, are left including Leo Kaplan in Manhattan, Lewis Wexler in Philadelphia, Tercera in California, and Pritam & Eames on Long Island. The halcyon days of the late 1980s and 1990s, when the Peter Joseph Gallery in New York created a buzz in the field and even paid retainers to struggling makers, seem to be gone forever.

Rather than sell though galleries, about a quarter of the makers market their work at craft shows such as those sponsored by the American Craft Council, the Baltimore Craft Show, the Smithsonian Craft Show, the Providence Fine Furniture and Furnishings Show, the Philadelphia Furniture and Furnishings Show, and others. Half again as many reported that they did a few shows early on in their careers. The craft show circuit is grueling, not only from the standpoint of having to make a body of furniture to display, but also because of the physical effort of setting up and manning the booth for four or five days at a time. After trying it once or twice, many makers quickly swore off it. For the best-known makers the craft show circuit is not necessary, but it has been a traditional avenue of entry for makers starting out. Furthermore, established makers often have teaching responsibilities that render the craft show routine impossible. Younger makers are not so encumbered, and the majority of those who do shows are full-time makers.

Some 20 percent sell furniture from their own showrooms, and a few state that customers can view work in their own homes. Many makers do not want the constant interruptions that walk-in customers cause. They would rather that clients deal indirectly, through galleries. Their shops are small and often located in remote areas or are shared with other makers, conditions not conducive to drop-in traffic. As an alternative to displaying their work in a showroom, at least 40 percent of the makers maintain Internet sites. A significant number are thinking of setting up a site or are actually in the process of designing Web pages. The response to these Web sites has been mixed, with some reporting good results and others none at all. As one alternative to showcasing their work on a Web site, more than three-fourths of the makers have succeeded in placing their work in museums, even if a significant number of these museums were only small local institutions.

Aesthetic Influences and Approaches

And finally, what does the furniture look like, what are the approaches, and what are the influences that shape the work? For the first generation of makers (ten in this survey) there was no question about their priorities. It is about the wood, about the techniques, and about the making. Tage Frid, first at the Rochester Institute of Technology and then at the Rhode Island School of Design, taught a whole generation of young makers that technique came first and really determined design. Many of his students, including John Dunnigan, Jere Osgood, and William Keyser, carry on this tradition in their own work and have passed these values on

top row, left to right: Slipper Chairs, John Dunnigan, 1990 (Renwick Gallery of the Smithsonian American Art Museum). *Points of Reference: Atlas, Webster & Roget,* Alphonse Mattia, 1995 (Renwick Gallery of the Smithsonian American Art Museum). *G.W. Cabinet,* Tommy Simpson, 1994 (Renwick Gallery of the Smithsonian American Art Museum). *Blanket Chest,* Mark Del Guidice, 2000.

bottom row, left to right: Sarcophagus Cabinet #1, Charles Radtke, 1999 (Renwick Gallery of the Smithsonian American Art Museum). *Blond Variables in a Canyon,* Brent Skidmore, 2003. *Side Chair,* Wendy Maruyama. *Primal Television,* Ed Zucca, 1994.

to another generation through their teaching. As a result, between a third and a half, or 39 percent, of the makers in the study fall into the category of first generation or first-generation interpreters.

Not surprisingly, among the 30 or so self-taught craftsmen in the survey, about 60 percent adopted the first generation, Scandinavian-influenced design approach emphasizing workmanship and materials. Indeed, many of these makers learned woodworking from the guides published by Tage Frid, James Krenov, and Sam Maloof. Charles Radtke is so focused on the wood that he actually cuts his own supply from locally available trees, saws and dries his own lumber, and slices his own veneers.

Related to the first-generation makers and interpreters in their emphasis on workmanship is a group of makers who focus on surface treatment. Of course, the first generation was horrified by the use of paint that covered up the figure of the wood, but in reality working the surface is just another technique to work the wood.[10] Representing about 8 percent of the field, this group lavishes untold hours on the surface. John Eric Byers meticulously paints each one-inch square on his furniture with five different coats of milk paint, spending up to 150 hours just for the surface treatment alone. Mark Del Guidice decorates his furniture with hieroglyphics, and on one chest summed up the labor-intensive nature

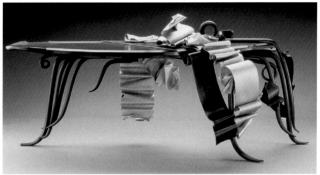

left to right: Large Demilune, Albert Paley, 1992. *No You Get Out of My Garden,* Paul Sasso, 1989. *At Ease,* Richard Ford. *Side Chair,* Victor Dinovi.

of the work by repeating in Morse code across the entire surface the mantra: "Labor of love, labor of love." Using South Sea carving techniques of the Maori tribes of New Zealand, Kristina Madsen embellishes her surfaces in such intricate detail that they look like the delicate lace she also enjoys making.

Another group of makers emphasizes material, but the material is not wood. Sometimes the furniture is a combination of wood and metal as in the work of Lee Schuette, Norman Peterson, and Chris Martin. Sometimes it is all metal as in the twisted steel shapes of Albert Paley, the smooth sculptural surfaces of Paul Freundt, or the jumble of metal rods and tubing that form the chairs by Eck Follen. Instead of steel, Peter Handler employs anodized aluminum for the frames of his upholstered chairs. Stephen Whittlesey assembles his furniture out of found wood as a way of recycling and preserving a bit of his New England environment. Sometimes it is wood gathered in the forest that is fashioned into the furniture of Clifton Montieth, or the found wood is combined with found objects as in the *Memory Series* of chairs by Daniel Mack. Jon Brooks starts with found wood too, but he meticulously smoothes and paints it with intricate squiggles and turns it into ladders, skinny dogs, and stick figures. Jim Syron and his partner, Bonnie Bishoff, work with polymer clay to create unique surfaces on their wooden frames. Charles Swanson has fashioned cabinets and tables in sharp-

edged, sculptural shapes with a thin plaster skin. Only 12 percent of the makers use alternate materials, but some of the most creative furniture is made possible with this experimentation.

Another 8 percent of the makers imbue their furniture with whimsy and wit. The top of Thomas Stender's *Wave Table* seems to wave good-bye as it turns into a gentle wave, and Richard Ford's brightly painted *At Ease Highboy* takes on the anthropomorphic stance of a military officer. Craig Nutt and David Ebner have fashioned furniture using the forms of garden vegetables. Joannne Shima's child's chair incorporates familiar icons of childhood with its Tinker Toy legs, Oreo cookies, and children's artwork on the back. More subtle is John McNaughton's latest series of convoluted houses, some bent into a U-shape and others that can be set on either end. Emi Ozawa's furniture has always conveyed a certain free spirit, but viewers are captivated by the intricate mechanisms designed to open and close her colorful boxes.

Sometimes overlapping with the whimsical is the narrative approach. Seventeen percent of makers use their work as a medium to tell a story. Rosanne Somerson's *Botanical Reading Couch,* now in the Renwick collection, recalls her childhood memories of sitting under a willow tree and reading. The tassels on the crest of one of John Dunnigan's *Slipper Chairs* suggest his gray hair while the piece of purpleheart on the other suggests his wife's red

left to right: All Mixed Up, Erik A. Wolken, 2001. *Dress Her Liquor Cabinet,* Jay Stanger.
Four Step Library Ladder, Dan Jackson, 1965 (Renwick Gallery of the Smithsonian
American Art Museum). *When She Was Bad Mirror,* Rosanne Somerson, 1995
(Renwick Gallery of the Smithsonian American Art Museum). *Broken Sphere Bench,*
Derek Secor Davis, 2000.

hair. Alphonse Mattia's *Step Vanities* conjure up the stuff his father once stored on the steps going down to the basement of his childhood home. Much of Tommy Simpson's work has an autobiographical component; his *G.W. Cabinet* alludes not only to the familiar story of George Washington and the cherry tree, but also to his own, less-than-happy experience playing George Washington in a sixth-grade play. Ed Zucca, master of the social comment in such work as his *Television Series,* plays off bygone eras against this icon of modernity.

And one last approach is purely sculptural where the work is about abstract shapes rather than figural representation. Even though he has reinvented himself numerous times, Wendell Castle mostly falls into the sculptural category: abstract, organic forms with varied and complex surface treatments. Brent Skidmore takes a similar approach, but his shapes are more slender and fragmented, and he marks the painted surfaces with raised geometrical knots.[11] In contrast to the rounded elements favored by Castle and Skidmore, Wendy Maruyama prefers sharp, elliptical shapes and paints them with a dark, rich palette. Derek Davis experiments with the geometry of balls, rectangles, and trapezoids to create pure sculpture that is still fully functional furniture. Almost 20 percent of the makers have adopted the abstract sculptural approach.

Only 25 percent saw a social or cultural content in their work. Gender issues dominated this approach with 11 respondents, notably Paul Sasso, Rosanne Somerson, and Jay Stanger. Political and religious themes were cited six and four times respectively. Several makers said, however, that they specifically avoided political and religious statements in order to present a positive and happy message. In an interesting interpretation of what a political statement meant, eight respondents pointed to an implicit message in their work of nobility, honesty, spirituality, and the desire to preserve hand-craftsmanship.

Whatever the approach—whether first-generation interpreter, narrative, whimsical, surface manipulation, or sculptural—all the makers were influenced to one degree or another by historical furniture, Modern art, or foreign cultures seen through travel. Art Nouveau in all its iterations— French, DeStijl, Vienna Secessionist, Antonio Gaudi in Spain and Charles Rennie Mackintosh in Scotland—was the most recognized influence at 34 out of 106.[12] The work by Victor Dinovi and Albert Paley most clearly draws on this source. Thirty-two people identified Jacques-Emile Ruhlmann and Art Deco as a major influence; Castle based an entire body of work on this source. The bulbous legs attached to the outside corners of case pieces refer directly to similar treatments

left to right: Table, Peter Handler. *Desk with Clock 2,* Wendell Castle, 1991 (Renwick Gallery of the Smithsonian American Art Museum). *(top) Stools,* Dean Pulver. *(bottom) The Drummer's Bench,* Andy Buck.

on much of Ruhlmann's work. Twenty-seven respondents pointed to the influence of Shaker furniture in their work. First-generation interpreters, particularly, were inspired by Shaker simplicity and fine craftsmanship. Japanese influence was also cited by 25 people who were responding to a similar simplicity in Japanese design. Many of the respondents also admired the high place that craftsmanship is accorded in Japanese society. Other styles frequently mentioned included ancient Egyptian furniture and decoration, African tribal art, eighteenth-century American and English furniture, the Arts and Crafts movement, and Scandinavian design from the 1940s and 1950s, particularly the work of Hans Wegner.

Modern art obviously had a major impact on the narrative, whimsical, and sculptural approaches to furniture design. For those such as Wendell Castle and J. B. Blunk, whose furniture took a free-flowing amorphous form, the sculptures of Henry Moore and Constantin Brancusi were obvious influences. Martin Puryear's handmade, biomorphic sculptures suggesting everyday objects often with overtones of African crafts were also singled out as an important influence, particularly on the work of Dean Pulver, Jon Brooks, Andy Buck, and Judy McKie. Cubism clearly is a component of the rectilinear and sharp-edged work of Eric Wolken, Wharton Esherick, and Joyce and Edgar Anderson.

Among the ten varied makers who cited Minimalism as an important influence were Peter Handler, Emi Ozawa, and Gail Fredell. Derek Davis, William Keyser, and John Dodd credited both Minimalism and Abstract Expressionism as important elements in their work. The Abstract Expressionist idea that art could express unconscious thoughts appealed to a diverse group of makers including Rosanne Somerson, Albert Paley, and Stephen Whittelsey.

Somewhat surprising given the lip service paid to Post-Modernism for its role in helping to free up design from the bonds of Modernism, only seven makers recognized this movement as a significant factor in their work. John Dunnigan acknowledged a direct impact in his rejection of Modernism and his desire to draw on past historical styles. The precariously perched *Hat Box Cabinets* of John Eric Byers also reflected the Post-Modernist belief in an unstable world. But Pop art, not Post-Modernism, informed the narrative work of Ed Zucca, Kim Kelzer, and Mitch Ryerson, who used found objects to tell their stories. Ryerson and several others also acknowledged the clear influence of Marcel Duchamp and his Readymades.

Roughly 72 percent of the makers had traveled outside the United States, although some did not feel that this exposure had much effect on their work. Some 14 makers recalled that travel around

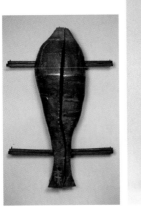

left to right: Swimmer, Stephen Whittlesey, 2004. *Hat Box Cabinet #2,* John Eric Byers, 1996 (Renwick Gallery of the Smithsonian American Art Museum). *Arm Chair Gardener,* Mitch Ryerson, 2000. *Home on the Range,* Kimberly Kelzer, 1991.

the country had a greater impact. Europe and South America were the most common destinations, but the influence of Scandinavia was disproportionate to the seven people actually traveling there. The furniture by Jere Osgood, Dan Jackson, and Robert Erickson shows the direct impact of their visits there, and of course, Tage Frid was born and trained in Denmark. The Japanese aesthetic is most apparent in the work of Michael Hurwitz and Thomas Hucker; John Cederquist's furniture also incorporates a strong Japanese component even though he never visited there. The Dominican Republic exerted a surprisingly strong influence, particularly in the choice of color in the work of Wendy Maruyama, Michael Hurwitz, and Randy Shull, after their sojourns at an artist colony on the island.

Trends in the Field

So what are the trends in the field? The most significant trend seems to be the introduction of the computer. The computer is gradually making inroads on both the drawing board for the production of plans and in the shop for the control of tools, particularly routers. The makers who have adopted the computer point out the efficiencies and the expanded possibilities this tool provides. Others, however, fear the loss of the maker's hand. As a sign of the times it is noteworthy that the computer was a major subject of the 2004 Furniture Society conference.

In terms of tools, only laser-cutting and vacuum-forming were cited as having any major new impact in the shop. It would not be practical for Thomas Stender, for example, to make his furniture in such complex shapes without the vacuum-forming technology. Laser-cutting has facilitated the wider use of metal in the field and also has sped up the tedious process of inlay work.

In the realm of design the most common refrain was "eclectic." No one could identify a single, dominant design trend comparable to the Post-Modernism of the 1980s and 1990s. Some people did see a reaction to Post-Modernism with a return to simplicity and a rediscovery of Scandinavian Modern and the simple lines of the Arts and Crafts Movement.[13] Others saw a trend toward even more personal expression. Chris Martin felt that furniture was becoming more cerebral and less functional, more like sculpture. Critics cautioned that if the work becomes too personal and too self-indulgent it will lose its universal appeal. The keepers of the craft tradition—Jere Osgood, Art Carpenter, and James Krenov—all agreed with that sentiment. And they would also lament the introduction of new materials such as metal, composites, and plastics, which have the potential for drastically altering design.

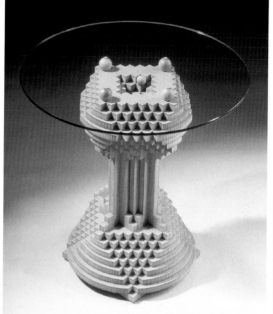

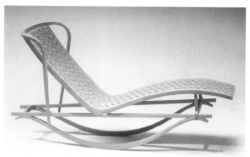

left to right: Rocking Chaise, Michael Hurwitz, 1992. *(top) Tashjian Chair,* Robert Erickson. *End Table,* Phillip Tennant, 1991. *Cabinet on Stand,* James Krenov, 2000 (College of the Redwoods).

Is the field prospering and getting bigger? A slight majority—37 percent, mostly the teachers—thought the field was getting bigger, but 31 percent believed it was becoming smaller or at least not growing. Another 31 percent said that they did not have a feel for what was going on in the field, reflecting perhaps the isolation of many makers. Many of the teachers at the major schools such as RIT and RISD identified a trend away from studio furniture and into industrial design or into pure art and sculpture. Alphonse Mattia at RISD estimated that perhaps two-thirds of his graduates were going into industrial design rather than solitary studio furniture work. He observed that this generation is not enamored of the romantic, counterculture notion from the 1970s of toiling away in their own shops and living on a shoestring.

The high cost of setting up a workshop is a major deterrent to entering the field. In the 1970s many studios opened in abandoned downtown warehouses where rent was cheap. With the urban renewal of the last few years and the back-to-the-city movement, cheap studio spaces have disappeared. The ever-increasing cost of tools presented another challenge. Even as the field appeared to be shrinking, several makers commented that craft shows seem to be attracting ever-growing audiences.

By many measures the field is prospering. More students than ever before are graduating from furniture programs, and the infrastructure such as the Internet, the Furniture Society, schools, museum collections, conferences, publications, and shows are all growing. However, galleries are one area that is contracting. But others observed that the gallery scene has always had its ups and downs.

At one extreme, Garry Knox Bennett declared that the field was "dead," adding that it had become "all glass and turning." On a more positive note, many makers felt that the public is better-educated today about the appeal of craft, and that as they compare industrial products with handwork the field will take off. Charles Radtke concluded that "as the baby boomers get older they will want personal expression items. They are more open-minded than the conservative generation of the 1950s." Phillip Tennant best summed up the state of the field: "Bigger, but slowly."

Notes

1. Although Edward S. Cook, Jr., Gerald W. R. Ward, and Kelly H. L'Ecuyer, *The Maker's Hand: American Studio Furniture, 1940-1990* (Boston: MFA Publications, 2003), makes a case for including Canadian craftsmen with the American counterparts, this study is limited to American makers with the exception of the emigré Peter Pierobon who lives in Vancouver, British Columbia.

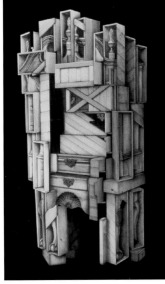

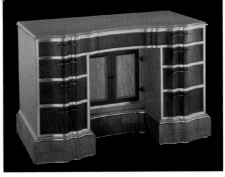
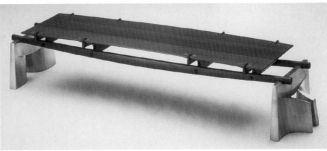

left to right: Ghost Boy, John Cederquist, 1992 (Renwick Gallery of the Smithsonian American Art Museum). *Kimono,* Thomas Stender. *(top) Boston Kneehole,* Garry Knox Bennett, 1989 (Renwick Gallery of the Smithsonian American Art Museum). *(bottom) Low Table,* Thomas Hucker, 1985 (Renwick Gallery of the Smithsonian American Art Museum).

2. In my list of 109 makers, one-fourth are not members of the Furniture Society. If we extrapolate from that figure to conclude that the 1,900 figure represents only three-fourths of the total number of makers than it is possible to calculate a conservative total of about 2,500—far too low according to people knowledgeable about the field. It would be most useful to substantiate a number in some way. Meanwhile, I've chosen to use an arbitrarily high figure of 20,000.

3. I am indebted to my son, Dr. Michael Fitzgerald, Associate Professor of Chemistry at Duke University, for making me aware of this technique that is commonly used in the scientific community.

4. She identified 78 books (13 of them catalogues published by the Peter Joseph Gallery) and 27 articles from *American Craft.* I supplemented her survey with 24 articles from *Woodwork* published between 1989 and 2004, 31 articles from *Fine Woodworking* between 1979 and 2004, and 5 articles from *American Craft/Craft Horizons* published before 1980. *The Maker's Hand* catalogue was also added since it had not been published when Johnson's study was completed. The mentions in these last publications only added to the number of publications of makers on the original list and did not result in any additions to the list.

5. I am grateful to Michael Monroe, Andrew Glasgow, Lewis Wexler, John Kelsey, and Marc Grainer for looking over my list and offering valuable suggestions.

6. Students in my American Studio Furniture class in the spring of 2003 completed 41 of the interviews including 20 by Marcee Craighill. I completed the rest, 65, as part of my 2004 Renwick Fellowship project.

7. I am indebted to Rosanne Somerson and John Dunnigan for providing information about Tage Frid who recently passed away after a long illness.

8. In the case of Wendy Maruyama and Charles Radtke, who have hearing impairments, it was more convenient for them to fill out a written questionnaire.

9. Eight received their BFAs from RIT, and of the fourteen makers who earned degrees from RISD all but two were MFAs.

10. Loy D. Martin, "Decoding Studio Furniture," in Rick Mastelli and John Kelsey (eds.) *Furniture Studio: Tradition in Contemporary Furniture* (Free Union, VA: The Furniture Society, 2001) pp.8-19 discusses the issue of labor in studio furniture and points to Garry Knox Bennett's watershed *Nail Cabinet* as an example

11. He uses an ancient Japanese technique to imprint the surface with various-shaped metal dies that crush the wood fibers. When water is applied the imprinted mark swells up above the surface of the wood.

12. The survey included 109 individuals but in three cases makers worked with partners: Beeken and Parson, Edgar and Joyce Anderson, and Bishoff and Syron. When issues concerning the work alone were considered, these partnerships were counted as one. Hence, the seeming discrepancy between 109 makers and 106.

13. A few observed that the popularity of the Arts and Crafts style may be due in large part to its rectilinearity and lack or ornament, making it easy to produce.

Considering the Pixel as a Beautiful Material

Though immaterial, it has the potential to become whatever the digital craftsman desires

by Paul C. Savino

I have big hands, apishly big hands for someone of my small frame. They are, however, sensitive hands. My life has been shaped by them and their capabilities. My hands have fed me, clothed me, defended me, silently told loved ones that I love them, shown respect for those whom I've held in high opinion, and disdain for others. But my hands are most capable as builders. This is why I am proud of them—despite the awkwardness of my body, I have the hands of a craftsman. They are at greatest ease when grasping a chisel or using a cabinet scraper to smooth a surface. A good day of work has ended when my hands are bloody and blistered.

Despite my holistic description of my hands, they are not conscious themselves; it is my intuition that gives them direction and motive. Between practicality and artistry, the choices made by the craftsman raise a piece from an object built out of necessity to one born from the love of technique and process. Craft is so often defined as skill. While true proficiency within a medium raises people to a level of great technical capability, it is their intent for the outcome of their labor, the enjoyment and understanding of their materials, and their willingness to harmonize these two, that aligns them with the ideals of craft.

This latter statement reflects a poeticized idea of craft, the view of a stoic workman whose heritage is fading in the modern world. Craft's vitality and

Paul Savino of Seattle submitted a version of this essay to the Cranbook Academy of Art while working toward a Master of Fine Arts degree.

practicality have been in question since the start of the Industrial Revolution. Until that point, consumers relied solely upon craftspeople for the production of their everyday goods. Even as recently as the early 1950s industrial production meant large groups of craftsmen working closely with designers and engineers in a factory setting. To the Modernist mind, the imperfection of human capabilities as builders makes people an undesirable

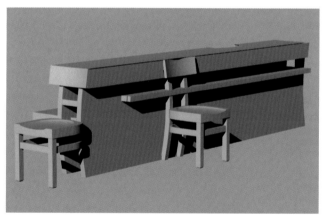

In conducting his digital exploration, Paul Savino derived 70 digital images from a single, rather plain chair. Some of them seemed suitable for actual construction, though most were less likely candidates.

component within the manufacturing process. And the necessity for goods in the marketplace has fueled the belief that handwork is a thing of artistry alone, not an economic component of or opponent to industrial manufacturing.

Thus has the practice of fine craftsmanship been relegated to a small group who either are capable of producing a modest living with their work or who accept craft as a hobby. Craftspeople are supported by a small market of the very wealthy and of those who enjoy the craft arts, and who are willing to spend money for handmade or unique goods. It is craft's ability to produce the unique and individual (even along a series) that gives it an edge over industrial manufacturing. This is not necessarily a superior edge, since well-designed and beautiful objects can be had by anyone these days, but the capacity for the creation of the unique object is something that industry has yet to capture.

In his book *Abstracting Craft: The Practiced Digital Hand*, Malcolm McCullough cites John Ruskin as stating in the *Seven Lamps of Architecture* (1849): "For it is not the material, but the absence of human labor, which makes the thing worthless; a piece of terra cotta or of plaster of Paris, which has been wrought by the human hand is worth all the stone in Carrara, cut by machinery. It is indeed possible, and even usual, for men to sink into machines

which instills a sort of Amish quality in much of their work, objects that are skillfully made but endowed with an aura of antagonism against technology. While the appreciation of historical techniques and traditions are paramount within the practice of craft, to rely solely upon them and thereby move against progress is to condemn oneself to creative stagnancy.

There is an opposite side to this spectrum and it has initiated a new discipline and level of discussion in digital craft. If our understanding of the computer is correct, then it is a tool. Perhaps it is a more complex tool than what we traditionally associate with the making of things, but it is a tool nonetheless. If we accept "tool" as a definition of "computer," then we must also accept that there is a group of devotees who are neither technicians nor designers. We must therefore broaden our definition of craft.

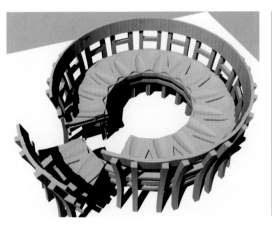 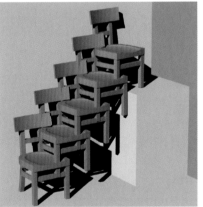 

themselves, so that even handwork has all the characters of mechanism." (McCullough 1996) Based on this, if a piece of terra cotta that has been shaped by man is worth all the machine-cut marble in Carrara, we must assume that this gesture, the intuitive movement of the artisan's hand, defines the nature of this discipline.

Is a pixel a product?

During my studies at Cranbrook, I was brought to amicable terms with something that I had once believed was the bane of craft: my computer. Many craft practitioners hold technology in contempt,

Sensory applications weigh heavily here—the feel of the materials, the way that tools react with them, the sensitivity one must have in the hands to interpret these reactions and respond to them. Our reliance on the hands is not merely a means to make work happen, but also a means to understand it. This is the importance of the gesture: to inform as well as to execute.

Sight is the second sense desirable to the practice of craft. Sight plays a great role in focusing on and understanding the nuances and formal qualities of materials while an object is being born from them, and sight plays an even greater role in the shaping of the crafted piece. While tactility offers a great deal of response and understanding, the craftsman recognizes visualization as the window of intent. Only those who understand the poetic nature of their medium can truly appreciate how to move through it and bring out its best. To enjoy a finish or the movement of grain or the flash of a raku glaze, to see what beauty you as a craftsman have made, is to love your work. Broken, tired, sweaty, and sometimes bleeding, if you cannot sample the visual richness of your completed labors and find solace in it, then your day was pointless.

So now we try to apply these things, senses, principles, to a cold beige box that was forged by a machine and that we do not sweat over, and yet, we do assign craft to it. It misses the tactility of materials completely, and it relies solely upon visualization to bring the maker gratification. We have control over its actions via a mouse or an electronic pen through a process called "direct manipulation" (a phrase coined in 1983 by the software designer Ben Shneiderman) that offers us no feedback since the "materials" being manipulated exist only in a virtual world. This seems a far cry from our understanding of craft. And yet, there are ideals within digital craft that do give a solid and passionate connection to the principles of craft, intent of use and intuition being the two strongest. While the technologies that can offer us a strong tactile connection to "materials" utilized by the computer-tool are still in their infancy, they will catch up and humanize the experience of creating physical objects in this way. But I would like to focus on the mental/spiritual intent of the digital craftsperson.

Let us try and visualize a pixel as the most beautiful and valuable material in the world. It is immaterial, so its use is harmless to the environment. No tropical rainforests are diminished, no mountains are strip-mined, no toxic chemicals result from its use. It is so full of kinetic energy that I wonder how it is contained within the beige box. It can be in motion, yes, an animated object, but more than that, it contains kinetic energy as it sits there, unmoving, because it has so much potential. It has

the potential to become whatever the digital craftsman desires. It can be any element, any substance, or any object, known or not yet realized. It is limitless information and therein lies its greatest capability. To have an understanding of, and control over, such a thing is a power that any truly proficient digital craftsman must relish. An infinite, completely abstract, completely universal material, one that will bend or yield to whatever its user/maker's intuition desires, whenever. The pixel can be difficult to use and entire projects can be lost faster than a chisel can slip. But with that in mind, the pixel is also the most forgiving and pliable material in the entire discipline of craft. Softer than clay, and firmer than steel.

So there is the love of the medium. Where is its context of use? What can be made of it, and for whose benefit? Our expectation for a physical object, hewn from the natural and then forged into the physical or tangible, is a mental barrier to understanding the digital object. The computer possesses a logic of which we cannot conceive. Though it is rational and based upon mathematical relationships, it also holds the possibility of the creation of abstract images and objects that might not retain the aura of the digital process through which they were conceived.

To illustrate these ideas, I constructed an archetypal chair form utilizing a digital mediator (3-dimensional modeling software) in the same manner as if I had built it out of wood. I attempted mutations of this chair in order to change its overall utility or perhaps to describe domestic furniture situations, elongating it to form a bench or chaise, mutating its legs to reproduce an additional chair form, creating group seating. And all of these variations, while yielding interesting forms in their own right, still contained the possibility of that which could be imagined and actualized without using the computer. Their language was prescribed and still recognizable. I was more interested in pursuing that which held a truly digital language, that which could not be realized outside of the computer, and utilizing the computer's capability to break it into components, without regard to the task of building it physically.

With my original chair at the center, I created a gridwork of digital distortions. Using the four most common tools of transformation contained within most 3-dimensional modeling software—bend, bloat, taper, and twist—each running along a different axis, and a mathematical equation to stimulate the changes, I created seventy new "chairs." While many of these were impossible to imagine as utilitarian objects, they contained some incredibly dynamic and gestural forms that could serve as either building blocks or as singular objects, all of which were imbued with the history and aura of at one point having been a chair.

All seventy of these virtual objects, while influenced by my decisions regarding which equation or transformation to use, were built by the computer's logic and infused with its digital language. The results are almost beyond comprehension. It is not about the user having expectations due to his mastery of a piece of equipment. It is about that piece of equipment's hyper-rationalization to create that which the user never could have conceived. It is a new machine aesthetic.

Modernism once streamlined and minimalized our objects, infusing them with a machine aesthetic based upon the technology of the time. With our contemporary capabilities and by melding domestic objects with current technology, we are seeing a recurrence of the Modernist ideal and a renaissance of the machine age. But unlike earlier methods of industrial production that were limited to mechanical process, digital technology has offered us a more fluid and organic process. Simple domestic objects can take on an aesthetic that is completely separate from, and not limited by, their own materiality. Imagine the display of information as neo-baroque, where surface can be ever-changing with style or trend, and the well-made object stands as an armature for the digital skin that covers it. A marriage of digital and physical techniques and an honoring of all materials used, pixel or otherwise, could yield fantastical ever-changing and long-standing results.

Contraposition Bench by Paul C. Savino, digital image created using Rhino 3D modeling software, actual bench constructed in cherry with ebony details, 2004.

Savino writes, "How is digital language translated into an actual physical object? What is gained and lost? Does it still hold the same meaning when constructed using traditional craft methods? The digital is something as organic and capable of variance in production as nature itself."

Digital craft is an entity separate from digital design. While both disciplines are meant to produce utilitarian images, interfaces, or objects, they utilize different means to their ends. Design weighs the socio-political effects of its objects' language on a different scale than that of craft. In opposition to this, craft focuses upon the poetic aspects of materials and the making processes that are applied to them, unique to each experience, in a way that design cannot consider (partly due to the scale on which it works and partly due to marketplace efficiencies). Design is meant for a mass market and mostly it yields products, not one-off objects. Craft is funded by those who can afford to have the highly individualized and unique luxury items that craftsmen produce. Perhaps digital craft in its current incarnation could be compared to digital painting, but that is a debate for those who enjoy parsing the differences between art and craft (expression vs. utility). As for me, I am more interested in using the digital to create the physical.

Lost in translation

If the creation of a physical object was directly linked to actions and gestures that occurred on a computer screen, so that it became a real-time process with those actions possibly producing an unexpected consequence, perhaps that would demonstrate the integrity of the computer's translation of the digital to the physical within a craft context. Rethinking the necessity for the physical and reserving material wealth for the most carefully conceived objects would demonstrate a true respect for the natural resources from which we craftsmen create our work. This is perhaps where the digital conception of objects benefits their analog creation the best.

McCullough describes in *Abstracting Craft* the proficiencies for physical realization that are offered to us by CADD/CAM technologies: "Thus, conversely to the widespread condition noted by the cultural critics, wherein things become images, here there occurs an inversion: thanks to CADD/CAM, and more controllability than ever before, images can become things." (McCullough 1996)

My skills as a maker doubled when I added the tools of conception and precision offered to me by 3-dimensional software. This enabled me to execute work of increased refinement and complexity. However, if one is to follow this process, where does the hand lie within the creative process? Is it in the digital conception of the objects? Is it the gesture of the mouse, the cunning eye and intellect that serves the digital craftsman alone, leaving the labor of fabrication to outside agents? If one is interested in digital craft alone, then this could be a viable means of producing work. However, just as craft has an ever-interjecting creative process, the changes that occur before and during the construction of an object could yield results not anticipated by the digital process. Material reactions, joinery details, just plain choosing to not stick with the drawing... these variables bring the creation of the physical to a level above the "fabrication of an already digitally crafted piece." Here, the fingerprints of the maker, the significance of being an integral part of an object's realization to its last coat of finish, and the celebration of the inevitable imperfections that result from our work, act not only as a demonstration of skill and expression, but also as testament to the poetry and honesty of craft—and to its persistence in the digital era.

Further Reading

Malcolm McCullough, *Abstracting Craft: The Practiced Digital Hand* (Cambridge, MA: The MIT Press) 1996.

David Pye, *The Nature and Art of Workmanship* (Bethel, CT: Cambium Press) 1968.

Steven Holtzman, *Digital Mantras* (Cambridge, MA: The MIT Press) 1994.

John Dunnigan, "Understanding Furniture," *Furniture Studio: The Heart of the Functional Arts*, pgs. 12–23 (Free Union, VA: The Furniture Society) 1999.

The Maker as Evidence

The Maker's Hand:
American Studio Furniture, 1940–1990

by Fo Wilson

The history that we retrieve is our interpretation of what happened, a myth or fiction that helps us explain how the world in which we live came to be.

—Jules David Prown, "In Pursuit of Culture: The Formal Language of Objects"
American Art 9, No. 2 (1995)

Jules Prown, a noted scholar, contends that history is fiction, limited versions of chronological orders of time, "small truths" that "build large untruths."[1] In his essay "Style as Evidence," he discusses the different philosophical approaches among historians of fine art, decorative art, society and culture, and the different methods they use to develop their versions of history. He articulates the differences in how these approaches view objects. Some treat them as ultimate subject matter. Others see objects as windows by which to view culture—another way of framing different outlooks towards form and content.[2]

Edward S. Cooke Jr., one of the curators of *The Maker's Hand: American Studio Furniture, 1940–1990,* points out that an object of furniture in different contexts can at once be a decorative art, an example of material or visual culture, design, or an object of art. Yet, each of these discrete disciplines functions in separate worlds with distinct criteria regarding how they are applied.[3] Oftentimes, these different approaches overlap into messy and confusing philosophical constellations. In many ways, the exhibition and catalogue for *The Maker's Hand* is a good example of some of the issues that plague art historical scholarship in general and

Fo Wilson is a graduate student in furniture at Rhode Island School of Design.

the study of contemporary furniture in particular.

In November of 2003, when the exhibition opened at the Museum of Fine Arts (MFA) in Boston, I walked through the galleries reveling in the opportunity to see this canonical work live and in living color. Though I was familiar with many of the pieces, I had only been able to see them in books. A dynamic range of examples by significant makers filled the show and captured seminal moments in its fifty-year span.

I wanted to play with Tommy Simpson's *Man Balancing a Feather on His Knows,*

The catalog for *The Maker's Hand: American Studio Furniture, 1940–1990,* ISBN 0878466622, published by the Museum of Fine Arts, Boston, is available through bookstores or from its distributor, DAP. The exhibition ran November 2003 through February 2004 and, unfortunately, did not travel.

and sit in Wendell Castle's monumental *Library Sculpture* to see if it was comfortable and whether I could carry on a successful conversation there. Like any other maker, I wanted to turn pieces upside down and open the doors and drawers to appreciate the technical virtuosity in work such as Wharton Esherick's table and chairs, or Jere Osgood's chest of drawers, and to run my hands along the leather upholstery of Vladimir Kagan's walnut lounge chair. I was tempted to engage with history (and annoy a guard or two) by touching the nail on Garry Knox Bennett's infamous *Nail Cabinet*. I am a graduate student in Rhode Island School of Design's (RISD) furniture program, so the show was also a back door into seeing and understanding more of my professors' work. Most of them are second-generation makers and some, carrying on the teaching tradition of their predecessor, the late Tage Frid, are reluctant to talk about or show their work to students, for fear of undue influence.

The exhibition and accompanying catalogue support to some degree the Furniture Society's goal of "fostering an understanding of [studio furniture] and its place in society."[4] At the very least they have spurred discourse and debate—from typical disagreements over the pieces and makers chosen for the exhibition, to arguments with the characterizations the curators chose to define each decade that the show covers.

Perhaps this exhibition's greatest gift was bringing this work into focus in the esteem of a museum setting through the ongoing commitment of the MFA. Having started its Department of Decorative Arts and Sculpture under the leadership of Jonathan L. Fairbanks in 1971, the museum is one of only a few institutions that have continually added contemporary studio furniture to its collections.[5] More than sixty-five thousand visitors[6] set their eyes on this work, and we can speculate that as a result these sixty-five thousand people might forever look differently at furniture.

Another contribution of *The Maker's Hand* is that by developing the catalogue and mounting the exhibition

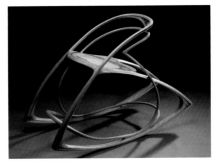

Delight Rocking Chair, Martha Rising, 1980.

at the MFA, it puts studio furniture in a larger historical framework and contributes to pushing insular debates about art, design, craft, and industry into a broader public sphere. Museum-goers and furniture collectors participated alongside makers and educators in a sold-out symposium, one of several activities held in January 2004 in conjunction with the show. In the months since the exhibition opened, I have also noted a rise in the number of articles in popular magazines such as *Dwell* about studio furniture makers, their work, and the rising auction prices of pieces by luminaries in the field.[7]

At the same time, it is how *The Maker's Hand* engages the larger historical framework that causes some concern. First off, the curators, Cooke along with Gerald W.R. Ward and contributions by Kelly H. L'Ecuyer, spend a good deal of time justifying their choice of the term studio furniture to categorize the work, yet they offer a fairly muddied definition. Through their many justifications they never do succinctly define it.

The 1989 catalogue for the MFA's first landmark exhibition in the field, *New American Furniture: Second Generation Studio Furnituremakers,* curated and written by Cooke, proceeds to lay out perhaps the first coherent genealogy of the evolution of studio furniture in America, and does so more concisely,

in my view, than what is presented in *The Maker's Hand.* Surprisingly here, Cooke defines studio furniture in an end note—a testament to how widely the term is accepted and used, but also how variously it can be defined and used.[8]

In the *New American Furniture* catalogue Cooke explains: "I use the term studio furniture since I find it the clearest term... Studio furniture is a more objective term since it conveys: an education based in the colleges rather than apprenticeship; the importance of a vigorous conceptual approach to design and construction, and the small scale of operation distinguished from factories or manufactories."[9] Obviously, to apply this definition to fifty years of making and makers, it had to be revised. *The Maker's Hand* was not only an opportunity to have a considered discussion about how we define studio furniture, but also to bring others into a broader, more public discourse around it—namely and most obviously the makers. Since so many of them are still alive and working, one can legitimately say the voice of the maker is as central and as critical an issue as any, in regards to historical documentation.

Benno M. Forman, the eminent decorative arts historian, discusses the challenges confronting historians in "Connoisseurship and Furniture History." He warns: "Things have a habit of becoming what we call them, and a name tends to become the definition of the object without explaining it."[10]

Herman Miller Chair, Charles Eames, 1946.

Peter Korn, executive director of The Center for Furniture Craftsmanship in Rockport, Maine, recently argued in the Furniture Society's newsletter that studio furniture is "furniture designed and built by individuals as a means of self-expression."[11] Tom Loeser, a celebrated maker and associate professor in the Department of Art at the University of Wisconsin—Madison, in the introduction to the catalogue for *Contemporary Studio Case Furniture: The Inside Story,* presents that show as pieces that "cannot be understood without an intellectual engagement with the ideas and intent of the maker."[12] John Dunnigan, RISD professor and maker, in his essay "Understanding Furniture,"

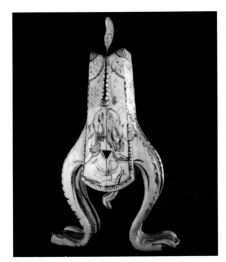

Man Balancing a Feather on His Knows, Tommy Simpson, 1968.

considers a definition that is dynamic. He asks that we understand furniture "as a material expression of the symbiotic relationships between technology, culture, style and the self."[13] Dunnigan inserts a dynamic in between the maker and the result—the relationship of the maker to the many different factors that influence his or her work. The self in particular is something that has been assumed by furniture scholarship, but not implicitly elaborated upon.

Dunnigan, Loeser, and Korn are just a few voices that suggest other dimensions not accounted for in the justifications and definitions of studio furniture in

Low-back Lounge Chair in Walnut and Leather, Vladimir Kagan, 1955.

The Maker's Hand. One of the intents stated by the curators was "to increase the understanding of the field for both the makers and the general public."[14] It seems that there is evidence of understanding on the part of the maker. Although we desperately need more voices of makers put on paper, there are enough to have been taken into account in the curators' efforts to further revise and clarify an evolving definition.

The show could have benefited in other ways from a more deliberate presence of the maker, notwithstanding their representative work and informative biographies, by reflecting on the experience of making that is as much a part of the work as the work itself. Dunnigan, in the aforementioned essay, tries to position studio furniture as more than the sum of its parts. He explains, "The maker may shape the object, but the object also shapes the maker."[15] This intimate experience with form and function, tools and materials, tactile and visual beauty, culture and self, is what connects furniture making to other artistic mediums and transcends the usual boundaries between craft and art. The best of studio furniture is different from other furniture classifications because of the effort by the maker to manipulate and push against the boundaries that make up the form, function, and language of furniture. Within this context, other discussions can begin to happen for studio furniture that are also suggested by its presence in the museum environment.

Through all the criticisms we might have, we can certainly applaud the curators' efforts in mounting this exhibition. What an ambitious and difficult job it must have been, to be faced with choosing and obtaining work to represent fifty years of studio furniture (however we define it). In reviewing the show we must also bear in mind that these respected historians operate within a scholarly tradition that comes with its own imperatives.

Decorative arts historians have traditionally approached furniture history as a chronological stylistic order plus a celebration of the technological mastery of the individual craftsperson. The need to define, categorize, formalize, and standardize the historical reading of objects can be an end unto itself. Historians become obsessed with filling in the blanks and finding a mark, that one bill of sale or letter that clues them in to an object's past life. Style, designation, periodization, provenance, and fictions developed around past tastes, are all part of a formal arsenal that freezes objects in time and discourages our perceptions from remaining fluid.

Cooke himself admits, in "The Long Shadow of William Morris: Paradigmatic Problems of Twentieth-Century American Furniture," that the current decorative arts canon is an "anachronistic fiction" of sorts that engages in a "technologically-obsessed formal study of one-off objects."[16] He feels that the legacy of the Arts & Crafts hero William Morris—who exalted the individual genius of the artisan and held contempt for mass production—is one of the factors that keeps decorative arts scholarships focused through a narrow lens.

In the case of *The Maker's Hand*, we also have the problem of trying to shoot a moving target. Present history is not standing still. History has taught us many times that a fixed position keeps us from realizing other potentials: the world is flat, you'll fall off. Of course that is a Philadelphia-made Chippendale, don't you see the shape

of the leg? The Western scholarly penchant to nail it in absolute terms can interfere with seeing all the possibilities.

Following studio furniture through the lineage of the decorative arts has no doubt affected what we see in it. As much as the catalogue and show try to expand the decorative arts purview by including a social context and quotes from makers, they don't break through a preoccupation with technique and materials to delve more deeply into object and form. Martha Rising's *Delight Rocking Chair* is one elegant and lyrical example of an expressive engagement with three-dimensional form and space. It develops the rocker form in ways that both carry on and evolve its historical precedents.

Much has been made of the fact that a good percentage of makers have come through university programs that contributed to their intellectual and conceptual rigor. Tommy Simpson, in talking about *Man Balancing a Feather on His Knows*, is quoted in the catalogue as saying, "I desire my furniture to depict storage as an adjective as well as a noun. I see an object which is for the safekeeping of goods take on meaning as the depository of hopes, loves, sorrows, as well as for books, foodstuffs, and underwear. Furniture can expand to receive more of [a person's] needs

Library Sculpture, Wendell Castle, 1965.

Pennsylvania Hill House Installation,
Wharton Esherick, 1940

than be just the handler of material."[17] It is quite profound that Simpson, originally trained as a painter at Cranbrook Academy of Art, would think at the time to imbue a piece of furniture with these qualities. Musings such as these are reported and documented as conceptual evidence, but rarely plumbed to any significant degree.

Perhaps there are different questions we can ask that are less about a compulsion to have to name or categorize studio furniture, and more about the need to know it. I agree with Korn when he suggests there might be something to gain in working from the maker forward, rather than from the object backward.[18] Starting with the maker brings to the fore the genesis of the work and opens a way to address the self.

The categorization used to define each of the five decades in *The Maker's Hand* is the criticism voiced most often by those in the studio furniture community. Though catchy, these oversimplifications don't serve the history of the field. When the fifth or sixth generation of makers look back they might be left with a confusing picture of how we defined the field, and an impression of what characterized the work of the first and second generations that doesn't reflect its true complexity. This exhibition represents one institution's interpretation, and we celebrate its contribution. As scholarship grows, I hope there is room for a myriad of

critical voices and that different ways of historicizing and reading studio furniture are explored.

Notes

1. Jules David Prown, "Truth of Material Culture: History or Fiction?" *Art as Evidence: Writings on Art and Material Culture* (New Haven, CT: Yale University Press, 2001), pg. 225.

2. In both "Style as Evidence" and "Mind in Matter: An Introduction to Material Culture Theory and Method," in *Art as Evidence: Writings on Art and Material Culture*, Prown discusses neoclassical readings of form as an engagement of eye and mind, whereas the material culturalist includes a physical, tactile experience of an object's past. He contends that the decorative arts is preoccupied with style more than content and that stylistic standards are a "shortcut to historical truth" (SAE pg. 66). He characterizes the Western conception of history as "man's increasing understanding and mastery of the physical environment, by the progressive triumph of mind over matter" (MIM pg. 71). Prown discusses how art history and archeology can be relevant to material studies and how these different disciplines and sub-fields overlap in methodology in some ways, but diverge philosophically and by purpose in others.

3. Cooke laments how studio furniture studies are held back from more progressive historical discourse by the legacy of William Morris, in "The Long Shadow of William Morris; Paradigmatic Problems of Twentieth-Century American Furniture," *American Furniture*, 2003. He says: "American scholars of Twentieth-Century material culture remain mired in the celebration of either individual craftspeople or designers and emphasize historical narrative at the expense of critical analysis or interpretation" (pg. 213).

4. Foreword by Andrew Glasgow in *The Maker's Hand: American Studio Furniture, 1940–1990* (Edward S. Cooke, Jr., Gerald W.R. Ward, Kelly L'Ecuyer. Boston: MFA Publications, Museum of Fine Arts Boston, 2003), pg. 7.

5. Under Fairbanks's leadership, the MFA in the mid-70s started the "Please Be Seated" program, which commissions work by prominent makers and has been successfully received by the public. Fairbanks gives a detailed accounting and discusses the department's history in depth in the introduction to *Collecting American Decorative Arts and Sculpture, 1971–1991* (Boston: Museum of Fine Arts Boston, 1991).

6. Conversation with Andrew Glasgow, June 16, 2004.

7. See *Dwell* magazine, June 2004, pg. 44; and September 2004, pg. 38.

8. Endnote #3, introduction to *New American Furniture: The Second Generation of Studio Furniture Makers* (Boston: Museum of Fine Arts Boston, 1989), pg. 28. In this essay Cooke discusses studio furniture as a convergence between art, design, and craft. In his essay "Defining the Field," from *Furniture Studio, The Heart of Functional Arts* (Free Union, VA: The Furniture Society, 1999), Cooke reiterated points from *New American Furniture*, much of which is reprinted in *The Maker's Hand*.

9. Ibid.

10. Benno M. Forman, "Connoisseurship and Furniture History," *American Seating Furniture, 1630–1730*. (New York: W.W. Norton, Winterthur, 1988), pg. 15.

11. Peter Korn, *Furniture Matters: The Furniture Society Newsletter*, (June 2004), pg. 9.

12. Virginia T. Boyd, Glenn Adamson, and Thomas Loeser, *Contemporary Studio Case Furniture: The Inside Story* (Madison, Wisconsin: Elvehjem Museum of Art, University of Wisconsin—Madison, 2002), pg. 10.

13. John Dunnigan, "Understanding Furniture," *Furniture Studio, The Heart of Functional Arts* (Free Union, VA: The Furniture Society, 1999) pg. 17.

14. *The Maker's Hand*, pg. 16.

15. See note 13 above.

16. See note 3 above.

17. Simpson, *The Maker's Hand*, pg. 44.

18. See note 11 above.

The Marriage of Decorative and Fine Art

Byrdcliffe: An American Arts and Crafts Colony

by Jonathan Binzen

A handful of the most eloquent cabinets of the Arts and Crafts era were produced in the well-equipped woodshop of an odd and largely dysfunctional art colony spread out on a hillside overlooking rural Woodstock, New York.

The colony's name, Byrdcliffe, was a compound of the middle names of its founders: an Englishman, Ralph Radcliffe Whitehead, and his American wife, Jane Byrd McCall Whitehead. Byrdcliffe's strengths and strangenesses were a reflection of the Whiteheads, a pair of aesthetically sensitive, upper-class romantics who sought the simple life at great expense—and never quite found it.

Furniture making at Byrdcliffe began with a burst of creativity. The colony opened in 1903 and within the first year and a half some fifty pieces of furniture—many of them large—had issued from the workshop. Produced through an unusual collaboration of craftsmen and artists, the pieces were distinguished by their pairing of sound, if staid, furniture forms with carved or painted decoration. In the most remarkable pieces, a series of stocky linen presses and several smaller cabinets, images of local flora or landscape were mounted as door panels framed by the rectilinear rails and stiles.

Jon Binzen of New Milford, CT, is a writer specializing in furniture and interiors. His most recent book, co-authored with Kevin Rodel, is Arts & Crafts Furniture: From Classic to Contemporary *(Newtown: Taunton Press, 2003).*

There was magic in the pairing; neither the cabinet designs nor the artworks were first-rate on their own, but they became compelling in combination. With these appealingly simple, utilitarian, tenderly ornamented cabinets, Byrdcliffe achieved one of the Arts and Crafts movement's fondest aspirations: a marriage on equal footing between decorative art and fine art.

And then that was it. By early 1905, Ralph Whitehead shut down the furniture shop. Other crafts—weaving, metalwork, and pottery, as well as painting and theater—continued to be practiced and taught at Byrdcliffe in

Linen Press with Sassafras Panels, Edna Walker, ca. 1904.

The Metropolitan Museum of Art, Purchase, Friends of the American Wing Fund, and Mr. and Mrs. Mark Willcox, Jr. Gift, 1991. (1991.311.1) Photograph ©1992 The Metropolitan Museum of Art.

more or less desultory fashion, but furniture was finished.

Whitehead had hoped that once he provided the initial investment the furniture shop would support itself. But whatever success he might have had getting the furniture designed and made, he never figured out how to sell it. Seven decades later, when Whitehead's son Peter died at White Pines, the family's Byrdcliffe residence, more than half of the woodshop's total output was found furnishing the rooms and hallways of the house.

• • •

These days we associate Woodstock with a more recent social experiment—Hendrix and macrame in the glorious mud, 1969—"Three days, man!" But any flower children who felt they were on an unprecedented adventure might have found it surprising to stop by Byrdcliffe that weekend. They might have felt a shiver of déjà vu amid the remains of an earlier experiment, one launched by a well-educated man who spurned the source of his family's wealth (though not the wealth itself) and sought more meaningful employment, apprenticing himself to a cabinetmaker or two; a man who believed in the morally transformative power of music, art, and hand work, and who spent much of his life trying to create a social and artistic enclave apart from society in accord with the lofty progressive ideals he locked onto in his twenties.

Ralph Whitehead was born in 1854 in Saddlebrook, England, and grew up in a stone mansion with a view of the Tame River and of the enormous woolen mills beside it that gave his family their fortune. Had he gone to Cambridge, he might well have followed his father and uncles in running the family business. As it happened he went to Oxford, where he came under the influence of the art critic and social theorist John Ruskin.

Ruskin's writings on the evils of industrialization, the improving power of manual work, and the moral dimensions of art and architecture were of prime importance for several generations, and became sacred texts of the Arts and Crafts movement. Inspired by the architecture and craftsmanship of Gothic cathedrals, Ruskin held up the medieval guild system of craft labor as a paradigm for the present. He felt that the whole man must be engaged in work and that divorcing manual from mental labor produced poor products and inhumane working conditions.

Whitehead embraced many of Ruskin's aesthetic and social prescriptions. One year, Whitehead returned from college and announced his intention to socialize the family factories. His family spurned the idea and packed him off to the Continent.

Whitehead's twenties and thirties are little-documented but seem to have been feckless years spent socializing in a string of villas and castles. Things changed when he met Jane Byrd McCall, a young and artistic American from a socially prominent family who was traveling in Europe with her mother and sister. McCall shared many of Whitehead's ideals and early on the two mapped out a life together that would bring their Ruskinian vision to fruition.

In 1892, after he shed his German first wife and married McCall, Whitehead and his bride moved to California. It was with artistic friends made in California and with others that Ralph met in Arts and Crafts circles in Chicago that the Whiteheads began to plan Byrdcliffe.

Whitehead's genuine affection for the arts, his devotion to the ideas of Ruskin and William Morris, and his willingness to underwrite an experiment in bringing them to life—these were like nectar to a range of creative, progressive people. Once the site was found and the buildings erected, Byrdcliffe was a hive of aesthetic activity in its first several years.

But Whitehead's generosity was twinned with an autocratic streak. However he

Byrdcliffe: An American Arts and Crafts Colony, ISBN 0964604205, Cornell University Press. An online version of the exhibition, with many photos and its travel schedule, can be found at www.museum.cornell.edu/byrdcliffe.

Byrdcliffe
An American Arts and Crafts Colony

tried to internalize them, the Ruskinian ideals of democracy and humility were always at odds with instincts for privilege and paternalism that were, for Whitehead, bred in the bone.

Whitehead's key recruits—among them the painter Bolton Brown and the writer Hervey White, who had helped select the site, design and build the buildings, and recruit the pioneers—left within a year or so. Byrdcliffe was crumbling even as it was being built.

Whitehead's internal ambivalence applied directly to furniture making. In a 1902 article laying out his concept for Byrdcliffe, Whitehead mentioned Ruskin and approvingly echoed his mentor, writing that "the joy of labor and the sanity of man depend on manual work done under healthy conditions." And that "art itself can never be strong and sane till the gulf which separated the artist from the mechanic has been bridged." In its brief flourishing, the Byrdcliffe furniture shop seems to have accomplished this, bringing cabinetmakers, carvers, and fine artists into fruitful collaboration. But Whitehead couldn't shake an

underlying mistrust of the common worker. In a letter, he wrote: "In order to have anything good made in stuff, or hard material, we must seek out the artist to provide us with a design, and then a workman to carry it out as mechanically as possible, because we know that if he puts any of his coarser self into it he will spoil it."

Within several years, Byrdcliffe became more a seasonal aesthetic resort than the community of working craftsmen and artists Whitehead had envisioned.

• • •

In the fall of 2001 I went to visit Byrdcliffe while researching a book on furniture of the Arts and Crafts movement. It was a ghostly place. The furniture shop was long gone, having burned to the ground some decades earlier. White Pines was eerily empty. Nearly all the furniture was gone; it had been inherited by a Whitehead cousin and much of it had since been sold off to museums and collectors. The plaster ceilings in White Pines were bulging and webbed with cracks, the original burlap wall coverings had come unglued and fluttered as you passed. The intentional modesty of the materials and woodwork gave the house an austerity that made it feel even emptier. One of the only rooms that held traces of habitation was up a steep, locked stairway in the attic. There, under the rafters, seemingly undisturbed, was a cramped studio where Ralph Whitehead poured himself into experimentation with pottery glazes after he failed to make a go of furniture and weaving. Of the twenty or so other Byrdcliffe buildings— including studios and workshops, houses, cottages, a dormitory, and a barn—nearly all were still standing, but many of them were empty.

• • •

Over the last twenty-five years a river of ink has been spilled in celebration and explication of the Arts and Crafts movement. Byrdcliffe's share of the spillage, however, has been barely a trickle. Now the flow has quickened.

"Byrdcliffe: An American Arts and Crafts Colony," an exhibition timed to the centennial of the colony's founding, provides the first comprehensive view of this curious endeavor. The show opened (inauspiciously, divided between several small venues) in Woodstock, NY, and then began traveling (in much expanded and far more impressive form) to the Milwaukee Art Museum and to Cornell University's Herbert F. Johnson Museum of Art in Ithaca, New York, among other sites.

The exhibition catalogue, *Byrdcliffe: An American Arts and Crafts Colony*, edited by Nancy E. Green, is rich with essays and images of life and craft and art at Byrdcliffe. The seven essays are anchored by Tom Wolf's lucid history of Byrdcliffe and his piece on the colony's artists, and by Nancy Green's careful delineation of Ralph Whitehead's upbringing and intellectual influences. Other pieces focus on Jane Whitehead as an artist (a rather thin subject), on Byrdcliffe's architecture, on its pottery, and on its furniture.

The essay on furniture—by Robert Edwards, a decorative arts dealer and sometime writer who has probably examined more Byrdcliffe furniture than anyone else—is very heavy going. Edwards fills the piece with pertinent facts, but fails to bring any order to them. Individual paragraphs are such a jumble of non-sequiturs they bring to mind a furniture maker who, lacking the patience to build a compartmented cabinet, stores all his tools in a sack. Stored thus, they have the advantage of being in one place, but...

The show's curators and essayists had a rich natural resource to work with: a wide range of people spent time at Byrdcliffe in its early years, and many of them recorded their impressions. Ralph and Jane Whitehead alone left a correspondence that runs to over 1,500 letters; they also left notebooks, calendars and paperwork related to the running of Byrdcliffe. In addition, there was an abundance of letter-writing and

autobiographical writing done by the stream of artists, craftspeople, writers, philosophers, naturalists, and vacationers who passed through Byrdcliffe. This trove of first-hand observation, a good bit of it now in the collection of the Winterthur library, forms the foundation of the catalogue and the show and brings to both of them an affectingly personal flavor.

Excerpts from letters, journals, and articles were featured extensively in the exhibit's wall texts, and in various parts of the show, audio tape loops played dramatic readings from them. The social spirit of a place is particularly ephemeral, but these readings, in concert with the many wonderful archival photographs, were surprisingly effective at evoking a certain mixture of idealism, self-seriousness, and open-hearted romanticism that evidently prevailed in the early days at Byrdcliffe. With the various tapes running simultaneously, however, the audio arrangement did inflict a bit of cacophony on the exhibition space.

The show brought together fifteen pieces of Byrdcliffe furniture—quite a feat considering that there are not many more than two dozen pieces known to be extant. There were also quite a few drawings directly related to the furniture, including presentation renderings, measured drawings, and studies for the decorative carvings and paintings. It was a treat to see the drawings displayed alongside the finished pieces—a practice many more furniture exhibitions ought to embrace—and it was particularly appropriate here since Byrdcliffe furniture represents the fusing of two-dimensional art with three-dimensional craft.

Despite the survival of an abundance of furniture-related paperwork and drawings, the exact authorship of Byrdcliffe's furniture remains somewhat murky. In most cases the artist responsible for designing the decoration of a piece is known, but the designer of the furniture itself is not.

Edwards suggests in his essay that Whitehead may have had his cabinetmakers model some of Byrdcliffe's furniture on pieces he saw in *The Studio*, an English magazine that featured many designers affiliated with the Arts and Crafts movement. Whatever their genesis, the better Byrdcliffe pieces have a winning modesty and directness that makes them exemplary partners for the decorative panels that adorn them.

Many of the decorative panels were designed by two talented young artists, Edna Walker and Zulma Steele, who found their way to Byrdcliffe from Brooklyn's Pratt Institute. In accord with Ruskinian principles (and no doubt at Whitehead's behest), they based their designs on close observation of plants growing in the immediate area. The plant shapes and habits were slightly stylized in the interests of composition.

The quality of the carvings ranged from quite impressive—in the case of some deeply modeled leaf carving by Giovanni Troccoli—to more the more technically pedestrian but still quite effective jigsawn relief patterns of many of the pieces.

The cabinets, too, were variable in the quality of their craftsmanship. Some have dovetailed drawers, others have drawers that are simply rabbeted and nailed. These are not finely made pieces; of very straightforward solid-wood construction, mostly in local woods, they are holding together well enough at a hundred years old, but the emphasis was on simplicity and utility rather than on technical flourishes or a polished presentation.

One group of pieces presented in the show takes the Byrdcliffe formula in a different direction with distinctly less satisfying results. Designed by the painter Dawson Dawson-Watson, the pieces are evidently based in form on Tyrolean furniture. Where the linen presses, for instance, are very soundly proportioned and simply detailed, these pieces—which include a settle and a blanket chest—are maladroit in form and decorated with somewhat heavy-handed jigsawn botanical relief patterns.

Byrdcliffe attracted an array of talented painters as teachers and students, especially in its first years, and the show was rich with their work. There were scores of works on canvas, panel and paper, and prints; in oil, watercolor, pen and ink, and charcoal. The paintings and drawings present no unified style—in fact, they are quite heterogeneous—but they do have in common a certain gentleness and a fondness for nature that accords with the Arts and Crafts movement.

The show also embraced quite a bit of ceramic work—some three dozen pieces—and there was a smaller section of metalware and jewelry, and some examples of weaving and book binding. There were appealing pieces to be found, but to be honest... not that

many. Here as elsewhere among Byrdcliffe's crafts output, truly accomplished pieces are rare.

• • •

With very few exceptions, those who stayed at Byrdcliffe didn't stay long. But even those who found Byrdcliffe or Whitehead disagreeable often found Woodstock irresistible. Many of Byrdcliffe's defectors (and happier veterans) settled nearby. Hervey White, whose talent for friendship had attracted many to Byrdcliffe, started a colony of his own, the Maverick. White and the Maverick, known for their bohemian bent and encouragement of music and theater, have had a lasting influence on the area. The gifted painter Birge Harrison, a close friend of the Whiteheads' who moved from California to teach at Byrdcliffe, stayed briefly and then left to found the

summer school of New York City's Art Student's League, locating it in Woodstock. It proved to be a very successful program and has attracted a steady flow of artists to the area ever since. Many others originally affiliated with Byrdcliffe played a part in turning the farm town of Woodstock into a mecca for artists, musicians, writers, and others of an artistic or politically progressive ilk.

Until the arrival of the current exhibition and its catalogue, this not-quite-intentional seeding of the surrounding community was Byrdcliffe's most tangible legacy. It may still be the most meaningful one, but now, with this careful examination of the intentions and accomplishments of the early denizens of Byrdcliffe, a far richer assessment can be made.

The Albatross of Functionality

Design≠Art *at the Cooper-Hewitt*

by John J. Curley

Cow Wallpaper, Andy Warhol, 1966.

With its exhibition "Design≠Art: Functional Objects from Donald Judd to Rachel Whiteread," the Cooper-Hewitt National Design Museum in New York has raised the old albatross of American postwar Modernism: that of functionality. Sol LeWitt's *Folding Screen* from 1986 (photo on facing page)—a room divider with a target design on its surface—cogently expresses these stakes. The target is not a neutral subject in this context, but one of American Modernism's most canonical motifs (think only of Jasper Johns and Kenneth Noland). When the screen is functional and not flat, the target's symmetry and

John J. Curley is a doctoral candidate in the Department of the History of Art at Yale University.

deductive structure are not visually available. Only when the screen is completely open—and not able to stand on its own—is the geometric gestalt of the picture realized. As a piece of furniture, *Folding Screen* feels incomplete, as if it is constantly striving to become a flat picture, and thus non-functional.[1] With its tension between pattern, decoration, and art, LeWitt's object revisits the American debates about wallpaper from the early postwar period, as does a small, concurrent sister exhibition at the Cooper-Hewitt called "Artists' Designed Wallpapers" (with examples by Andy Warhol and others). Considering both exhibitions, it is clear that functionality has been an issue in American Modernism since at least the late 1940s.

Wallpaper was a key critical term in the early days of abstract expressionism: the two primary spokesmen for American painting, Clement Greenberg and Harold Rosenberg, both used the word

Folding Screen, Sol Lewitt, 1986.

as an asymptote of sorts in their divergent definitions of what constituted a successful canvas. In 1952, Rosenberg defined "action painting" as a large-scale, performative type of abstraction; as both large and non-figurative, these works could cross over into something like "apocalyptic wallpaper" if the artist was not careful.[2] Alternatively, Greenberg believed that a good canvas should approach the condition of decoration—flatly expanding infinitely like wallpaper—but must also transcend this decorative function.[3] So while both critics justified their appreciation of an artist like Jackson Pollock with different criteria (Rosenberg's dramatic confrontation vs. Greenberg's quiet contemplation), they each suggested painting's visual affinity with decoration and its supremacy over it. *Design≠Art* expresses the continuation of such a functional unconscious in American Modernism, notably through the furniture of Donald Judd on display.[4] Instead of showing connections between advanced painting and wallpaper, this exhibition shows the continuing evolution of the relationship

between art and function by displaying a number of objects that reveal the connections between 1960s sculpture and furniture.

While the "Design≠Art" exhibition alludes to this tension between art and functionality, it is not adequately theorized as such. This complex and knotty problem could have been the exhibition's *raison d'etre;* instead it is a secondary concern addressed only through out-of-context quotes on gallery walls, a provocative title, and an essay in the catalogue.[5] And most importantly: How can visitors ponder the art/design problem when presented with only the design work of these visual artists? If the curators had explored larger juxtapositions for these objects—first, displaying the art objects by the artists, and second, the design and fine art production of designers and craftsmen—they could have offered a compelling alternative history of the 1960s–1990s. With their visual rhymes, a classic Judd box on the floor next to one of his desks featured in the exhibition would have been an informative comparison, as would the presence of both functional and non-functional potted vessels by someone like Peter Volkous, a craftsman sometimes discussed in the same terms as Pollock in the late 1950s and 1960s.[6]

While the very title of the exhibition promises to investigate the relationship of art and design, the overall display contradicted such noble intentions—especially since visitors could not touch, much less use, the objects. Additionally, with such a one-sided tale of production on view, the show creates the suspicion that furniture made by famous artists is worthy of display based on name

recognition alone. To be considered as serious poetry, for instance, the poems of a novelist should be considered with other contemporary verse, as well as in the narrower context of the author's novels. Without such a broad consideration, the poems of a novelist can be of formal interest in terms of the poems themselves, but not to any discussion about breaking down artistic barriers between genres. "Design≠Art" suffers from a similar limitation.

That being said, certain objects in the exhibition do call attention to the ambiguous, tortured nature of the relationship between art and functionality. The functional *Daybed* (1999) (photo on following page), by the British artist Rachel Whiteread, turns the cast of the space underneath a bed into a bed itself—thereby literalizing the domestic and functional allusions of her sculpture. By offering a comfortable functionality, the intense melancholy associated with her typical sculpture (usually concrete or plaster casts of such voids as the space inside a room or underneath a chair) is somewhat alleviated. This conflict between loss and acquired function adds a new dimension to her work. Alternatively, without the supporting context of his canonical works of the late 1960s (bits of shaped, dyed canvas

Design ≠ Art: Functional Objects from Donald Judd to Rachel Whiteread, ISBN 1858942667, Merrell Publishers.

The Nature of the Gun, Richard Tuttle, 1990.

pinned to walls), Richard Tuttle's gargantuan room environment *The Nature of the Gun* (1990) is hard to consider broadly, especially since his later, more furniture-like artworks are not well known. As with most of the other objects in the exhibition, visitors are also not told for what context Tuttle made this set (was it for himself, for sale in a design store, or for gallery exhibition?) and in what quantity they were produced (mass-produced or unique objects?). These omissions preclude a serious consideration of the art/design dynamic.

Roberta Smith writes in her recent New York Times review that the figure of Donald Judd looms over "Design≠Art"

Rachel Whiteread, *Daybed,* 1999

the "way Picasso would over a survey of Cubism."[7] Not only is Judd the most represented artist in the exhibition, but his works also best demonstrate the dogged persistence of functionality within American artistic Modernism. Like Whiteread, Judd's furniture pieces echo his art, with one critic commenting that they "are so close in spirit and form to his sculptures, that is difficult to define the distinction, except to acknowledge the utilitarian aspect."[8] Back in 1967, in looking at Judd's artwork, Greenberg came to a similar conclusion, saying that his Minimalist sculpture is more akin to "Good Design" than to art.[9] If one comes to the exhibition with prior knowledge of Judd's sculpture and his related

writings, then his desks and chairs can communicate the contradictions inherent in the relationship between art and design, in spite of the exhibition's serious shortcomings.

Judd's seminal 1965 essay "Specific Objects" is indebted to Greenberg's theories of painting, but the artist stretches the critic's ideas to a breaking point.[10] Greenberg believed in a gradual refinement of painting's protocols in order to explore the essence of the medium. This included the promotion of pictorial flatness and the abandonment of traditional, perspectival illusionism. While Judd was also against such effects in art, he goes further than Greenberg by claiming that all painting created such spatial illusions—be it a flat monochrome or a realistic landscape. As a remedy, Judd suggested that art should employ actual industrial materials in real space and use symmetry and mathematical ratios to escape pictorial illusionism. By applying Greenberg's ideas to actual materials in the viewer's space, Judd constructs a version of the critic's theories for the third dimension—one that must be viewed in relation to furniture, not wallpaper.[11]

In writing about Minimalist sculpture as "Good Design," Greenberg at once acknowledged and disparaged the furniture-like quality of Judd's sculpture. Nevertheless, in the mid-1960s this slippage between art and non-art was a quality Judd desired:

> The forms of art and of non-art have always been connected; their occurrences shouldn't be separated as they have been. More or less, the separation is due to collecting and connoisseurship, from which art history developed. It is better to consider art and non-art one thing and make the distinctions one of degree.[12]

Judd's 1969 *Untitled* is a highly polished, anodized aluminum box—open-ended on both sides, its interior lined with purple Plexiglas. Although executed before Judd's direct engagement with furniture, *Untitled* does clearly allude to the form of a table. At thirty-three inches tall, it is a reasonable height for a table, while its open ends would even allow for leg room. But this piece does something that most furniture does not: it wreaks havoc on the viewer's perception. When looking through the piece, the translucent Plexiglas reflects light in a way that produces an apparent fogginess within the void of the work—and even creates the appearance (however false) of a clear Plexiglas barrier covering the other open end.[13] A number of critics have highlighted the interplay of "allusion and illusion" in Judd's works, despite the artist's avowed intention to create only "specific objects."[14] In many ways, it is this illusionism that captures these objects for fine art. Even though Michael Fried dismissed Judd's sculpture in 1967 as "theatrical" (needing a

viewer to complete it), it can nevertheless fulfill some of Fried's rigid prescriptions about art. In some ways, *Untitled*'s illusionism allows it to transcend its own metallic, table-like objecthood—ultimately transforming it into a complex object investigating human perception.[15] As critics in the 1950s viewed Pollock's painting as going beyond wallpaper, one could say something similar about Judd's sculpture in relation to furniture.

But just as *Untitled* recalls a table, his furniture also exhibits illusionary qualities. His *Chair #48* from 1984 (photo on p. 122) is fashioned from highly reflective copper. The seat comes close to visually evaporating in its semi-closed nexus of reflecting light—where it is difficult to discern its real joints from reflected ones in the infinite regress of its three shiny sides. Additionally, its outward-facing flanks reflect and inflect its environment, optically fusing this chair into its surroundings. His massive *Desk #74* from 1990 (photo below) also creates perceptual play with its protruding, grid-like structure and recessing voids—its effect comparable to an exaggerated, regularized version of Rodin's

Desk #74, Donald Judd, 1990.

expressive bump-and-hollow technique. Furthermore, the actual writing surface of Judd's desk appears to be hovering largely unsupported, a structural technique that Judd also used in a number of his sculptures.[16]

In 1992, after fifteen years of making furniture, Judd wrote the essay "It's Hard to Find a Good Lamp" (reproduced in the Cooper-Hewitt exhibition catalogue). In a tone befitting a manifesto, this essay renounces the artist's earlier stance of blurring the division between art and non-art by clearly erecting a Greenberg-like barrier between the two fields of art and furniture:

> The configuration and the scale of art cannot be transposed into furniture and architecture. The intent of art is different from that of the latter, which must be functional. If a chair or a building is not functional, if it appears to be only art, it is ridiculous. ...A work of art exists as itself; a chair exists as a chair itself."[17]

So where does Judd's changing perspective on art and furniture leave us? By playing both sides, he certainly exemplifies the tension between the two. But, like many artists before him, Judd's practice eventually tries to escape the ambiguity between what was perceived as art and non-art, between the perceptions of sculpture and furniture. A look at his practice will help explain why.

To return momentarily to Jackson Pollock, T. J. Clark has argued that the violence and obsessive scrawling associated with the artist's "gothic" painting of the mid-to-late 1940s like *Full Fathom Five* became too sublimated and aerated by 1950 in the canonical drip paintings like

Chair #48, Donald Judd, 1984.

Autumn Rhythm.[18] For Clark, the decorative fact of the paintings (when the earlier dissonance turned into something too aesthetic) became clear to Pollock in 1950 when *Vogue* magazine used several canvases as backdrops for a Cecil Beaton fashion shoot. Clark calls this colonization of the avant-garde "the bad dream of Modernism;"[19] this is the moment when an artist fails to hold the contradictions and tensions of Modernism in check. And it is around this time when Pollock attempts to halt such appropriation by reverting to the dark figurative painting of his late work.[20]

In contrast, "It's Hard to Find a Good Lamp" exposes Judd's desire to erode distinctions between art and functionality visually, but it also shows how he carefully avoids the consequences of this radical, postmodern practice in his writings. He produces both art-like furniture and furniture-like art, but he does not want these overlapping practices to jeopardize his standing as a modern artist whose sculptures transcend the

everyday realm of function. Where Pollock shifted his practice, Judd only changed his writings. Judd's choice of language in the above quote is telling: he claims his intentions are different when producing furniture—thus allowing for a subjective differentiation of two things that actually look quite similar. Even taking Judd at his word, it's clear that the more he refined his furniture and the more he searched for the essence of sculpture, the more these different products looked the same. Just as the form of his sculpture belies the non-illusionism outlined in his writings, Judd's furniture cannot be viewed as a separate enterprise from his sculpture, no matter how much he protests.

The question becomes, why would Judd make such an artificial division in his writing that did not visually exist? In the catalogue to the exhibition, Barbara Bloemink rightly suggests that Judd's explicit separation might have something to do with protecting the reception and high prices of his sculptures, while still retaining his ability to make and sell expensive furniture.[21] This assertion exposes another largely unacknowledged presence in the exhibition: the market. Like Judd, "Design≠Art" also wanted it both ways. By showing these objects divorced from their dialogue with fine art and without the trappings of functionality (use, marketing, price, patrons), the exhibition presented functional goods as fine art, without impinging upon the "aura" of fine art.[22] While I certainly would not exclude artist-designed furniture from discussions of fine art, such dialogues should always question the very existence of categories in the first place,

and explore the motives behind such rigid divisions.

Minimal art was deeply engaged with the political and economic structures of the 1960s, mainly in its relation to the shift from the mass-consumption model of the 1950s to the more flexible model of the following decade that allowed for and, indeed, colonized individual subjectivity. In his 1960s sculptures, Judd used the materials of mass production—steel, plywood, Plexiglas, and particleboard—in order to call attention to the spectator's own changing and embodied perception. By forcing viewers to look and perceive in time, the objects offered perceptive feedback and an acknowledgement of the viewers' own bodies, despite the machine-made look of the art. A shift in marketing in the 1960s followed a similar logic; advertisers no longer spoke to the masses in what has been termed late capitalism, but to individuals.[23] One has to think only of the famous campaign by Volkswagen from the 1960s in which the Beetle was positioned as an alternative to the mass culture, despite its mass-produced ubiquity and tainted history of Nazi complicity. Thus, as the 1960s continued, Minimalism's model of subjectivity became complicit in a shifting corporate culture.[24]

The marketing and public availability of Judd's furniture (and many other objects in the Cooper-Hewitt exhibition) does not begin until the 1980s, the so-called "me decade" when the art market enjoyed its greatest prosperity to date. This connection between the artists' production and economic cycles can help me articulate a relation between Judd's simple furniture forms and the late capitalist consumer. Writing in the immediate wake of the 1980s, Rosalind Krauss argues that Minimal art had transformed the art museum into a site of spectacle—a transcendent locale outside of historicity where one's experience of space, not art objects, becomes primary.[25] Minimalist objects enable such feelings by dramatizing and

Donald Judd, *Spring Street Sink and Shelf,* 1970–71.

activating space through their industrial materials and large scale.[26]

In some ways, Minimalist objects transmute their own self-awareness to the surrounding space. Judd's art-like furniture can endow its domestic space with some of the cachet of a modern museum, as it too activates its surroundings. What is crucial here is the visual function of Judd's furniture—how it looks in a room, how it functions domestically like three-dimensional paintings or wallpaper. If opulence was the way to show status at Louis XIV's Versailles, the self-reflexive awareness of Judd's furniture might be seen as the new gilt and mirrors for the converted SoHo lofts of the 1980s. Through their form, Judd's desks and chairs can show off domestic space, and, by extension, the people who occupy it. As such, Judd's furniture turned the interior of the Gilded Age Carnegie mansion, which now houses the Cooper-Hewitt, into the star of "Design≠Art." Reversing Modernism's white cube strategy of emphasizing a work of art by surrounding it with neutral walls,[27] a Judd chair can emphasize the walls (and the rest of the interior space) and

its sitter. The presence of a Judd bench in the Calvin Klein flagship store in New York demonstrates this relationship between art, capital, and marketing. The function of Judd's furniture is not so much chair-ness, but status and lifestyle—something that also comes across when considering its high price.[28]

Judd's furniture even repels human use in many ways. With its unforgiving copper, its lack of contours, and its dangerously sharp corners, *Chair #48* is not very enticing. In fact, it looks more like a small bookcase. Furthermore, a number of his bookcases in the exhibition stymie effective use because of the metal or wood planks blocking full access to the shelves. The market for art had finally evolved to where a piece of furniture's lack of utility, comfort, and finish could be transformed into assets and signifiers of status.

Be it wallpaper or furniture, a "functional unconscious" has haunted postwar American Modernism. It has affected art's very forms, but also has been damned as inferior. With the emphasis on both functionality and fine art in "Design≠Art" one more specter needs to be addressed: Marcel Duchamp. His 1913 notion of the "readymade"—as noted in the exhibition catalogue—transforms a bottle rack into a valuable work of art, thus stripping away its function.[29] But Duchamp also created "reciprocal readymades," a lesser-known, and decidedly more radical, operation. In this process, Duchamp would endow "auratic" fine art objects with functionality, thereby negating their status and monetary value—using a Rembrandt as an ironing board being his most famous example.[30] As it is, "Design≠Art" is indebted to only one side of Duchamp's balanced practice of the readymade: it elevates functional goods to the status of fine art (with its attendant

monetary value), while still keeping art/design distinctions for the most part intact (not allowing for the tainting of art with function). The show also could have offered visitors the other, more problematic side of the equation. 🪑

Notes

Thanks is due to Morna O'Neill for reading a draft of this essay and offering valuable suggestions. And I would also like to acknowledge Professor Edward Cooke and Ethan Lasser's Decorative Arts Reading Group at Yale for encouraging dialogues between the histories of art, craft, and design.

1. LeWitt's *Folding Screen* is also in dialogue with another practice of the artist: his wall drawings that he began in the early 1980s. These also feature the iconography of geometric shapes, but are painted directly on walls by LeWitt's assistants. When the drawing is sold, there is a transfer of an ownership certificate; his assistants then paint over the "original" drawing; and finally they repaint the drawing in a different location for the new owners. Because LeWitt liberates these wall drawings from any site-specific context, they allude to a decorative function that is similar to wallpaper.

2. Harold Rosenberg, "The American Action Painters," *Art News* 51:8 (December 1952), p. 49.

3. Clement Greenberg, "The Crisis of the Easel Picture" (1948), reprinted in Clement Greenberg: *The Collected Essays, vol. 2, Arrogant Purpose,* ed. John O'Brian (Chicago: University of Chicago Press, 1986), pp. 222-3. In addition, Jackson Pollock's first large scale work, *Mural* (1943-44), was the result of a specific decorative request of Peggy Guggenheim for her New York apartment. Her decorative needs, in some ways, allowed Pollock to realize the aesthetic power inherent in a monumental/decorative scale. See Thomas Crow, "Fashioning the New York School," in *Modernism in the Mass*

Culture (New Haven: Yale University Press, 1996), pp. 39-48.

4. My term of the "functional unconscious" borrows its syntax from Rosalind Krauss' notion of the "optical unconscious." See Rosalind Krauss, *The Optical Unconscious* (Cambridge, MA: the MIT Press, 1993)

5. In contrast to the exhibition itself, Barbara Bloemink does address the relationship between the art works and functional objects in her exhibition catalogue essay. While a good start, her interpretation of this relationship does not situate this relationship historically. The debate is not static, and its changing manifestations (say, Russian Constructivism in 1920s Russia versus Donald Judd furniture in 1980s America) must be viewed in light of the changing social, political and cultural structures. See Barbara Bloemink, "On the Relationship between Art and Design," *Design≠Art: Functional Objects from Donald Judd to Rachel Whiteread* (London: Merrell, 2004), pp. 2-154.

6. For example, see Rose Slivka, "The New Ceramic Presence," *Craft Horizons* 21:4 (July/August 1961), pp. 30-37.

7. Roberta Smith, "Designers for a Day: Sculptors Take a Turn," *New York Times*, September 10 2004, E2, E25.

8. Erika Lederman, "Donald Judd Furniture," *Art Monthly* 184 (March 1995), p. 45.

9. Clement Greenberg, "Recentness of Sculpture" (1967), reprinted in *Clement Greenberg: The Collected Essays, vol. 4, Modernism with a Vengeance*, ed. John O'Brian (Chicago: University of Chicago Press, 1993), p. 256. Art historian James Meyer also views Judd's furniture as similar to his sculpture. See his *Minimalism: Art and Polemics in the Sixties* (New Haven: Yale University Press, 2001), pp. 220-1.

10. Meyer, *Minimalism*, pp. 134-41. For Judd's original text see Donald Judd, "Specific Objects," *Arts Yearbook* 8 (1965), pp. 74-82.

11. Greenberg's criticism was too attached to painting and its *a priori* autonomy to appreciate Judd's text or his sculpture. While the critic did occasionally praise sculpture (David Smith and Anthony Caro, for example), his admiration was often expressed in painterly terms.

12. Judd, "Month in Review," *Arts Magazine* 39:1 (October 1964), p. 64. He was writing about the "Twentieth Century Engineering" exhibition at the Museum of Modern Art, New York.

13. Of course, this effect cannot be seen in a photographic reproduction. I saw this sculpture in March 2004 at a Judd exhibition at London's Tate Modern.

14. Rosalind Krauss, "Allusion and Illusion in Donald Judd" *Artforum* 4:9 (May 1966), pp. 24-26.

15. Michael Fried, "Art and Objecthood," *Artforum* 5:10 (June 1967), pp. 12-23. Of course, other parts of Fried's critique of Minimalism certainly do apply to Judd—how, for example, the experience of a Judd sculpture exists in time.

16. Bloemink, p. 46.

17. Donald Judd, "It's Hard to Find a Good Lamp" (1992), reprinted in *Design≠Art: Functional Objects from Donald Judd to Rachel Whiteread* (London: Merrell, 2004), p. 189.

18. T.J. Clark, *A Farewell to an Idea: Episodes from a History of Modernism* (New Haven: Yale University Press, 1999), pp. 342-3.

19. Ibid., p. 306.

20. Ibid., pp. 365-6.

21. Bloemink, p. 48. Bloemink, however, does not discuss the contradictions or the temporal lapse between Judd's two positions on furniture (mid-1960s and 1990s). Such a difference demands to be interpreted via changes in the art world and in the socioeconomic realm.

22. I borrow the term "aura" from inter-war social critic Walter Benjamin, which

he defines as the quality of fine art derived from its traditions of singularity, rarity, and site-specificity. See Walter Benjamin, "The Work of Art in the Age of Mechanical Reproduction" (1936), in *Illuminations*, ed. Hannah Arendt, translated by Harry Zohn (London: Fontana Press, 1973), p. 215.

23. For a cunning discussion of 1960s advertising, see Thomas Frank, *The Conquest of Cool: Business Culture, Counterculture, and the Rise of Hip Consumerism* (Chicago: University of Chicago Press, 1997).

24. Elsewhere, I have labeled this Janus-like position of Minimal art the "social crux" of Minimalism, after Hal Foster's "crux of minimalism." See Hal Foster, "The Crux of Minimalism" in Howard Singerman, ed., *Individuals: A Selected History of Contemporary Art 1945-86* (New York: Abbeville Press, 1986), pp. 162-182.

25. Krauss, "The Cultural Logic of the Late Capitalist Museum," *October* 54 (Fall 1990), p. 7.

26. Ibid., pp. 4, 8.

27. See Brian O'Doherty, *Inside the White Cube: The Ideology of the Gallery Space* (Santa Monica, CA: Lapis Press, 1976).

28. Judd acknowledges the high prices of his furniture in "It's Hard To Find a Good Lamp," p. 193.

29. Bloemink, pp. 20-21.

30. Marcel Duchamp, "Apropos of Readymades," *Art and Artists* 1:4 (July 1966), p. 47. Duchamp never enacted this transformation of a Rembrandt painting. Donald Judd was interested in Duchamp and owned a later version of one of his "ready-mades"—the hanging snow shovel entitled *In Advance of the Broken Arm* (original 1915). See Bloemink, p. 21.

Unveiling the Renwick's Riches

Right At Home: American Studio Furniture

by Glenn Adamson

As devotees of the studio furniture movement flocked to the Renwick Gallery's 2004 survey of their field, they may have had somewhat mixed feelings. The furniture junkie's heart may have swelled with pride, enthusiasm, and eagerness at the prospect of the show. The approach to the museum could not be grander, as the Renwick is a stately old building located right on Pennsylvania Avenue across the street from the White House. Since opening in 1972, it has done justice to its real estate, staging numerous path-breaking exhibitions

the rare major exhibitions in our field. And what can it mean that the museum selected the exhibition title "Right At Home: American Studio Furniture," which claims for the field nothing more ambitious than cheery domesticity? (In case there were any doubts on this score, the main introductory label for the show finishes with the line: "Perhaps there is something in this exhibition that would be right at home in your house;" textile

in the exhibition itself, which is a straightforward and satisfying unveiling of the Renwick's riches. Categories like New Classicism, Metal and Fiber, Sculpture, Scandinavian Modern, and Color and Finish serve to divide the galleries into rough groupings. These are not parallel or systematic in relation to one another, and don't add much to the proceedings, but they don't distract much either, and give some anchors to those visitors who may be untutored in the key organizing ideas of the field. There are certainly much better things to command the viewer's attention than display arrangement, in any case: this is among the largest shows of studio furniture in history, clocking in with nearly sixty examples. If it is not quite definitive in the manner of the recent survey "The Maker's Hand" at the

Oops!,
Jacob Cress, 2001

Landscape of My Mind,
Norma Minkowitz, 1976-8

Ghost Clock,
Wendell Castle, 1985

Chair,
Shinichi Miyazaki, 1975

Music Rack,
Richard R. John, 1975

with the prestigious backing of its parent institution, the Smithsonian American Art Museum (SAAM). Its craft collection is among the largest and best in the nation, and its curators have included some of the leading lights in the field. A nearly complete view of the Renwick's furniture holdings is therefore an occasion for celebration.

On the other hand, the object selected as the image for the show's banners was Jacob Cress's *Oops!* It is disheartening that the Renwick thought it best to use this slight amusement—a Chippendale chair with cartoon eyes, in which a claw foot grasps wildly after its wayward ball—as the signature object for one of

hangings by major artists such as Olga de Amaral, Lia Cook, and Mariska Karasz are placed decoratively on the gallery walls, in a further misjudged gesture toward *gemütlichkeit*.) This is the fourth in a series of five media-themed shows focusing on the museum's craft collection, which began with "Glass! Glorious Glass!" in 2000, continued with "USA Clay" and "Jewels and Gems," and will finish with "High Fiber" in 2005. In this sequence of titles the phrase "Right at Home" seems, well, right at home, part of a program intended to frame craft as a consumer digestible.

Fortunately, this disappointingly anti-intellectual packaging is not reflected

Boston Museum of Fine Arts, the cross-section is quite varied and includes more pleasant surprises than predictable canonical examples. The breadth of the Renwick show can be attributed to the varied personalities of the Renwick's curatorial staff over the years—Lloyd Herman, Michael Monroe, Jeremy Adamson (no relation to this reviewer),

Glenn Adamson is curator at the Chipstone Foundation in Milwaukee. In that capacity he curates exhibitions at the Milwaukee Art Museum and teaches at the University of Wisconsin, Madison. Many of the pieces mentioned in this review are shown on pages 92 to 105.

and Kenneth Trapp. On the basis of accession dates it is possible to trace the growth of the collection according to each curator's tenure.

Lloyd Herman made most of his furniture acquisitions in 1975, a banner year in which his exhibition "Craft Multiples" led to the acquisition of more than sixty pieces in all media. Herman's

Desk, Wharton Esherick, 1950

shopping spree means that the present show has embedded within it a time capsule of a moment when the studio furniture world was expanding rapidly. This is a great chance to see work by lesser-known but worthy figures such as Richard R. John, Robert Whitley, and Shinichi Miyazaki. Also dating to this period is an early John Cederquist, in which the master of illusionary façade was still building funky wall cabinets composed of finely made shelves mounted on leather-covered pipe forms. Perhaps the least expected and most wonderful work from the 1970s is a chair entitled *Landscape of My Mind* by the fiber artist Norma Minkowitz, which is made of heaped-up cotton and silk over a wood frame.

Michael Monroe, who came to the Renwick as associate curator in 1974 and later became curator in charge, made the strongest group of acquisitions in the institution's history. It is to his credit that he pursued a relatively conservative strategy, finding historical material for the collection instead of shopping for what was being made at the moment. This is a classic demonstration of the

fact that hindsight is 20/20: by focusing on early work by established leaders of the field, Monroe was able to premise his choices on proven importance rather than personal impulse. Unsurprisingly his acquisitions form the backbone of the show, ranging from individual masterpieces like Wendell Castle's 1985 *Ghost Clock* and Rory McCarthy's unbelievably complex dining table of 1976 to representative examples by Tage Frid, Rosanne Somerson, Tom Loeser, and Tommy Simpson. (Two of his most important acquisitions, John Cederquist's cabinet entitled *Ghost Boy* (page 105), and Judy McKie's iconic *Monkey Settee* (page 96), given in Monroe's honor by the James Renwick Alliance, were not included in the show because they are currently traveling in the Renwick exhibit "Masters of Their Craft.") Monroe also benefited from the landmark Boston Museum of Fine Arts exhibition "New American Furniture," in which contemporary makers responded to antique forms. The show traveled to the Renwick and several of the best works entered the collection, including examples by Garry Knox Bennett, Michael Hurwitz, and Jere Osgood.

Kenneth Trapp became curator-in-charge at the Renwick in 1995 and stayed until 2003. Perhaps liberated by the canonical work that Monroe had conducted before him, he set about bringing color, life, and humor to the collection. Though Trapp's tastes and my own do not coincide, there is no doubt that he put an enviably populist topspin on the institution. Baroque constructions like Kim Schmahmann's *Bureau of Bureaucracy,* a curious cabinet with marquetry depicting such things as a book titled "Humanity" falling off a shelf, and Stephen Courtney's *Secretarial Desk,* topped with an arcing layer of golf tees, are typical of his acquisitions, as are the bright cartoon furniture of Richard Ford and Joanne Shima. The selection of the Cress chair as the show's

logo object is perhaps the final expression of this whimsical, elbow-in-the-ribs aesthetic. Yet not all of Trapp's selections tend to excess. Among the most ravishing objects in the show are a finely carved and upholstered side chair by Kristina Madsen and a beautiful piece of cabinetmaking by Charles Radtke (page 99). From Bob Trotman comes a truly unsettling set of library steps entitled *Louise,* in which the user has to climb up on the back of an over-life-sized female clerical worker (page 93). A few historically important objects came in on Trapp's watch, including a set of Dan Jackson library steps and an early Garry Knox Bennett bench made of unpainted fir; and a strong grouping of Sam Maloof pieces also came into the collection in the late 1990s, as a result of senior curator Jeremy Adamson's tremendously impressive retrospective on the California furniture maker. But on the whole, Trapp pursued a risky course during his stint at the Renwick, preferring to keep his finger on the pulse of the moment rather than backfilling with historically proven examples. While it is likely that his acquisitions will not all stand the test of time in the way that Monroe's have, it is also probable that future generations of historians will be glad that Trapp so fully captured our own eclectic moment.

In the end, of course, a permanent collection exhibition is an inherently scattershot exercise, as much the product of happenstance opportunity as coherent planning. It is a tribute to the Renwick's past leadership that this exhibition is as strong as it is; and, more importantly perhaps, a tribute to the furniture movement itself that the work on view is so rewarding. This is one show that belies its own title: these pieces of furniture fully deserve the spotlight they received in Washington. They are right at home after all—right at home, that is, on the platforms of the Smithsonian Institution. ♪

Index

For working designers, the digital camera has become an essential addition to the sketchbook. This table setting installation at Kew Gardens, England, was captured by furniture maker Tom Loeser and included in his presentation entitled "Fifty-Nine Cool Things" at The Furniture Society's 2004 conference.